KT-210-168

KiDS'
Party Cakes

KiDS'
party Cakes

THE AUSTRALIAN
Women's Weekly

ConTenTs

Indicates that a pattern for the
cake is included in this book.
Pattern sheets are in the pocket
at the back of the book.

welcome to the party

Can you recall the wiggles of anticipation you felt as a child, snuggled in bed at night, as it grew closer and closer to your birthday?

Do you remember dreaming up, choosing, asking for certain special birthday cakes? Changing your mind, checking with friends, scouring through magazines and cookbooks for the *perfect* cake?

Well, guess what? Some things never change (thank goodness), and kids today still have the same wishes, wants and dreams... different manifestations maybe, but still zeroing in on universal birthday cake themes of fantasy, favourites and fun.

Some of the best presents are our childhood memories: make your child's birthday-cake picture come to life and watch them smile.

itty bits of individuality

critters & crawlers

CAKE

340g packet
   buttercake mix
1½ quantities butter
   cream (page 206)
orange, blue, pink,
   green, dark blue and
   yellow colouring

1 Preheat oven to moderate.
Line 12-hole (⅓-cup/80ml)
muffin pan with paper patty
cases. Make cake according
to directions on packet,
pour ¼ cup of mixture
into each hole; bake in
moderate oven about
20 minutes. Stand cakes
in pan 5 minutes; turn
onto wire rack to cool.

2 Divide butter cream among
six small bowls. Tint each
bowl of butter cream with
one of the suggested colours:
orange, blue, pink, green,
dark blue and yellow.

TIP The buttercake mix and the butter cream
are enough to make 12 patty cakes. Decorate the
remaining six patty cakes with your own favourite
critters and crawlers.

DECORATIONS

Each quantity is enough for one patty cake.

CREEPY CATERPILLAR

6 orange Runts
   or M&M's
2 spearmint leaves
black glossy
   decorating gel

CRAWLY SPIDER

1 giant Jaffa
1 Jaffa
1 black licorice strap
black glossy
   decorating gel

BUTTERFLY BEAUTY

2 yellow jelly beans
4 chocolate freckles
2 yellow Crazy Bananas
black glossy
   decorating gel

DRAGONFLY

3 raspberries
4 strawberries and
   creams
2 Jelly Tots
black glossy
   decorating gel
2 orange Crazy Bananas

TINY TURTLE

1 green gum ball
2 green Runts or M&M's
1 green Oompa
2 spearmint leaves
black glossy
   decorating gel
red glossy decorating gel

BUZZY BEE

3 black jelly beans
2 yellow Crazy Bananas
1 black licorice strap
white glossy
   decorating gel

CREEPY CATERPILLAR

Spread some of the yellow
butter cream over one patty
cake. Position orange Runts
on cake for body. Split
spearmint leaves in half
through centre; position
for leaves. Using black
decorating gel, dot eyes
and mouth on caterpillar.

CRAWLY SPIDER

Spread some of the green
butter cream over one patty
cake. Position giant Jaffa for
body; position Jaffa for head.
Cut licorice into thin strips,
cut eight 3cm pieces from
licorice strips; position for
legs. Using black decorating
gel, dot eyes on head and
draw line on back of spider.

BUTTERFLY BEAUTY

Spread some of the blue
butter cream over one patty
cake. Position yellow jelly
beans for body; position
freckles for wings. Position
Crazy Bananas for antennae.
Using black decorating gel,
dot eyes on butterfly.

DRAGONFLY

Spread some of the dark blue
butter cream over one patty
cake. Position raspberries for
body; position strawberries
and creams for wings. Trim
Jelly Tots for eyes, use a little
butter cream to position on
front raspberry. Using black
decorating gel, dot pupils on
Jelly Tots. Position Crazy
Bananas for antennae.

TINY TURTLE

Spread some of the pink
butter cream over one patty
cake. Position gum ball for
shell; position Runts for tail.
Position Oompa for head;
position spearmint leaves
for flippers. Using black
decorating gel, dot spots on
shell; using red decorating
gel, dot eyes on turtle.

BUZZY BEE

Spread some of the orange
butter cream over one patty
cake. Position black jelly
beans and Crazy Bananas
alternately for body. Cut
wings from licorice strap.
Using white decorating gel,
pipe parallel lines on wings;
position on either side of
body. Cut 1cm piece from
licorice strap, cut into thin
pieces; position for pincers.
Using white decorating gel,
dot eyes on bee.

little Cakes of hOrror

CAKE

340g packet
  buttercake mix
1½ quantities butter
  cream (page 206)
green, red, black and
  blue colouring

1 Preheat oven to moderate.
  Line 12-hole (⅓-cup/80ml)
  muffin pan with paper patty
  cases. Make cake according
  to directions on packet, pour
  ¼ cup mixture into each hole;
  bake in moderate oven about
  20 minutes. Stand cakes in
  pan 5 minutes; turn onto wire
  rack to cool.

2 Divide butter cream among
  six small bowls.

TIP The buttercake mix and butter cream are enough to
make 12 patty cakes. Decorate the remaining six patty
cakes with your own favourite little cakes of horror.

DECORATIONS

Each quantity is enough for one patty cake.

SNAKES ALIVE

7 Brite Crawlers
black glossy
  decorating gel

GHOULISH GHOSTS

2 milk bottles
black glossy
  decorating gel

WACKY WITCH

1 black and orange
  licorice allsort
2 orange mini M&M's
1 orange Crazy Banana
black glossy
  decorating gel

GRUESOME EYEBALL

1 large white
  marshmallow
1 black Smartie
white glossy
  decorating gel

BLACK CAT

1 brown Smartie
1 brown mini M&M
1 black licorice strap
1 yellow Crazy Banana
3 yellow cake
  decorating stars
white glossy
  decorating gel
black glossy
  decorating gel

BAT ATTACK

1 black jelly bean
1 black licorice strap
white glossy
  decorating gel
black glossy
  decorating gel
3 white cake
  decorating stars

SNAKES ALIVE

Cut 1.5cm deep hollow from
centre of one patty cake. Tint
one bowl of the butter cream
with green colouring; spread
some of the butter cream over
hollowed cake. Position ends of
Brite Crawlers in hollow. Using
black decorating gel, dot eyes
on snakes.

GHOULISH GHOSTS

Tint one bowl of the butter
cream with black colouring;
spread some of the butter
cream over one patty cake.
Cut milk bottles into ghost
shapes; position on cake. Using
black decorating gel, dot eyes
on ghosts.

WACKY WITCH

Reserve 1 tablespoon of butter
cream from small bowl. Tint
remaining butter cream with red
colouring; spread some of the
butter cream over one patty
cake. Slice a thin strip off allsort,
trim into triangle; position for
witch's hat. Using remainder of
allsort, cut black pieces into two
thin strips; position on cake for
hat brim. Position M&M's for
eyes; position Crazy Banana for
nose. Tint reserved butter cream
with green colouring. Spoon into
piping bag (page 209); pipe hair
onto witch. Using black
decorating gel, dot pupils, nose
bump and mouth
on witch.

GRUESOME EYEBALL

Tint one bowl of the butter
cream with red colouring;
spread some of the butter
cream over one patty cake.
Trim top
of marshmallow; centre on
cake for white of eye. Position
Smartie on marshmallow for
pupil. Use white decorating
gel to pipe veins around
white of eye on
red butter cream.

BLACK CAT

Tint one bowl of the butter
cream with blue colouring;
spread some of the butter
cream over one patty cake.
Position Smartie on cake for
cat's body and mini M&M for
head. Cut small piece of
licorice strap into thin strip;
position on body for tail. Cut
small piece of licorice strap
into two small triangles;
position on head for ears.
Position Crazy Banana on
blue butter cream for moon;
position stars around moon.
Using white decorating gel,
pipe eyes on cat; using black
decorating gel, dot pupils
on eyes.

BAT ATTACK

Tint one bowl of the butter
cream with red colouring;
spread some of the butter
cream over one patty cake.
Centre jelly bean for bat's
body. Cut two wings from
licorice strap; position on
either side of body. Using
white decorating gel, pipe
clouds on red butter cream
for sky and eyes on bat;
using black decorating gel,
dot pupils on eyes. Position
stars on red butter cream.

animals

CAKE

340g packet
  buttercake mix
1½ quantities butter
  cream (page 206)
black, pink, brown and
  orange colouring

1 Preheat oven to moderate.
Line 12-hole (⅓-cup/80ml)
muffin pan with paper patty
cases. Make cake according
to directions on packet,
pour ¼ cup mixture into
each hole; bake in moderate
oven about 20 minutes.
Stand cakes in pan 5 minutes;
turn onto wire rack to cool.

2 Place one-third of the butter
cream in small bowl; tint
brown. Divide remaining
butter cream among four
small bowls. Leave one bowl
of butter cream white; tint
one of the remaining bowls
with black colouring to make
grey. Tint remaining two
bowls pink and orange.

TIP The buttercake mix and butter cream are enough
to make 12 patty cakes. Decorate the remaining six
patty cakes with your own favourite animal cakes.

DECORATIONS

Each quantity is enough for one patty cake.

ERNIE ELEPHANT
2 Mint Slices
2 purple Fizzers
black glossy
  decorating gel
5cm piece black
  licorice rope
2 yellow Crazy Bananas

CUDDLY BEAR
3 white chocolate Melts
black glossy
  decorating gel
1 brown mini M&M
2 white Choc Bits
1 red jube
2 teaspoons Coco Pops

TERRY TIGER
1 black licorice strap
2 green mini M&M's
1 black jelly bean
1 red mini M&M
1 black and orange
  licorice allsort
black glossy
  decorating gel

PRISCILLA PIG
2 pink marshmallows
2 blue Smarties
2 pink mini M&M's
1 pink Musk Stick

KITTY CAT
1 black and pink
  licorice allsort
black glossy
  decorating gel
1 black licorice strap
2 yellow jelly beans
1 pink mini M&M

DEEFA DOG
2 yellow Fizzers
black glossy
  decorating gel
3cm piece black
  licorice rope
1 mini red M&M
2 Clinkers

ERNIE ELEPHANT
Spread some of the grey
butter cream over one patty
cake and flat sides of Mint
Slices. Position Mint Slices,
butter cream-side up, for
ears. Position Fizzers for
eyes; using black decorating
gel, dot pupils on Fizzers.
Position licorice for trunk and
Crazy Bananas for tusks.

CUDDLY BEAR
Spread some of the brown
butter cream over one patty
cake. Position white chocolate
Melts for ears and nose. Using
a little of the black decorating
gel, secure M&M onto nose.
Position white Choc Bits for
eyes. Cut jube in shape of
mouth; position cut-side up
for mouth. Press Coco Pops
onto butter cream for fur. Using
black decorating gel, dot
pupils onto white Choc Bits.

TERRY TIGER
Spread some of the orange
butter cream over one patty
cake. Cut 10 thin slices on an
angle from licorice strap for
stripes. Cut two thin strips
for mouth. Position green
M&M's for eyes, jelly bean
for nose, licorice for stripes
and mouth, and red M&M
for tongue. Trim orange and
black layers from licorice
allsort, cut out two triangles to
form ears. Secure orange layer
onto black layer with a little
black decorating gel; allow
to dry then position on cake.
Using black decorating gel,
pipe lines on eyes for pupils.

PRISCILLA PIG
Spread some of the pink
butter cream over one patty
cake. Cut both marshmallows
in half horizontally and trim
the base of two for ears;
position on cake. Place one of
the remaining marshmallows,
cut-side up, on face for snout.
Position Smarties for eyes.
Secure M&M's on snout for
nostrils. Cut Musk Stick
lengthways into thin strips;
position for hair and mouth.

KITTY CAT
Spread some of the plain
butter cream over one patty
cake. Trim pink and black
layers from licorice allsort,
cut out two triangles to form
ears. Secure pink layer onto
black layer with a little black
decorating gel; allow to dry
then position on cake. Cut
thin strips from licorice strap
for whiskers and mouth, and
a triangle for nose; position
on cake. Position jelly beans
on cake for eyes; using black
decorating gel, pipe lines
on eyes for pupils. Position
M&M for tongue.

DEEFA DOG
Spread some of the brown
butter cream over one patty
cake. Position Fizzers for
eyes; using black decorating
gel, dot pupils inside Fizzers.
Cut licorice to form hair, nose
and mouth; position on cake.
Position M&M for tongue
and Clinkers for ears.

more animals

CAKE

340g packet
   buttercake mix
1½ quantities butter
   cream (page 206)
mauve, brown, red,
   green, black and
   yellow colouring

1 Preheat oven to moderate.
Line 12-hole (⅓-cup/80ml)
muffin pan with paper patty
cases. Make cake according
to directions on packet, pour
¼ cup mixture into each
hole; bake in moderate oven
about 20 minutes. Stand
cakes in pan 5 minutes;
turn onto wire rack to cool.

2 Divide butter cream among
six bowls; tint one bowl
with black colouring to make
grey, tint remaining bowls
mauve, red, brown, green
and yellow.

TIP The buttercake mix and butter cream are enough
to make 12 patty cakes. Decorate the remaining six
patty cakes with your own favourite animal cakes.

DECORATIONS

Each quantity is enough for one patty cake.

RANDOLPH RABBIT
2 strawberries and
   creams
2 pink Smarties
1 pink mini M&M
2 white Tic Tacs
1 black licorice strap
blue glossy
   decorating gel

LADYBIRD
1 black licorice strap
10 blue mini M&M's
white glossy
   decorating gel

KANDY KOALA
2 white chocolate Melts
2 pink mini M&M's
2 green Fizzers
1 large black jelly bean
black glossy
   decorating gel

MISS BEAR
2 milk chocolate Melts
1 Dairy Milk round
3 brown mini M&M's
1 pink licorice allsort
1 tablespoon chocolate
   sprinkles
1 black licorice strap
black glossy
   decorating gel

FIGARO FROG
1 white Mallow Bake
1 pink Smartie
2 brown mini M&M's

FELICITY FISH
1 orange crescent-
   shaped jube
2 purple jelly beans
1 orange mini M&M
25 white Choc Bits

RANDOLPH RABBIT
Spread some of the mauve
butter cream over one patty
cake. Position strawberries
and creams for ears. Position
Smarties for eyes, M&M for
nose and Tic Tacs for teeth.
Cut licorice strap into thin
strips and position for mouth
and whiskers. Using blue
decorating gel, pipe pupils
onto eyes.

LADYBIRD
Spread some of the red butter
cream over one patty cake.
Cut a half-moon shape from
licorice strap and position for
head. Cut licorice into a thin
strip; position on body for
wings. Position M&M's for
spots. Use white decorating
gel to dot eyes onto front
of head.

KANDY KOALA
Spread some of the grey
butter cream over one
patty cake. Position white
chocolate Melts for ears
and M&M's for inner ears.
Position Fizzers for eyes and
jelly bean for nose. Using
black decorating gel, pipe
dots onto eyes for pupils.

MISS BEAR
Spread some of the brown
butter cream all over one
patty cake. Position milk
chocolate Melts for ears,
Dairy Milk round for nose
and two M&M's for eyes.
Using a little of the butter
cream, secure remaining
M&M on nose. Trim pink
layer from allsort, cut into
two equal-sized triangles;
position for bow. Carefully
sprinkle chocolate sprinkles
over face for fur. Cut licorice
strap into thin strip for mouth.
Using black decorating gel,
pipe dots onto eyes for pupils.

FIGARO FROG
Cut small slit in front of one
patty cake for mouth. Spread
a little of the brown butter
cream inside mouth. Spread
some of the green butter
cream over top of patty cake.
Cut Mallow Bake in half;
position on frog for eyes,
position Smartie for tongue.
Use a little butter cream to
secure M&M's for pupils.

FELICITY FISH
Spread some of the yellow
butter cream over one patty
cake. Cut orange jube in half
horizontally, then in half
vertically; position for fins
and tail. Position purple jelly
beans for mouth and orange
M&M for eye. Position white
Choc Bits for scales.

even more animals

CAKE

340g packet
    buttercake mix
1½ quantities butter
    cream (page 206)
black, green, yellow and
    brown colouring

1 Preheat oven to moderate.
Grease 12-hole (⅓-cup/80ml)
muffin pan. Make cake
according to directions on
packet, pour ¼ cup mixture
into each hole; bake in
moderate oven about
20 minutes. Stand cakes
in pan 5 minutes; turn
onto wire rack to cool.

2 Leave one-third of the
butter cream white.
Divide remaining butter
cream among four small
bowls. Tint with one of
the suggested colours:
black, green, yellow
and brown.

TIP The buttercake mix and butter cream are enough
to make 12 patty cakes. Decorate the remaining six
patty cakes with your own favourite animal cakes.

DECORATIONS

Each quantity is enough for one patty cake.

RED BACK SPIDER

2 tablespoons
    desiccated coconut
black colouring
1 black licorice strap
4 red Skittles
2 purple Skittles
black glossy
    decorating gel

TOMMY TORTOISE

6 chocolate freckles
1 yellow jube
black glossy
    decorating gel
4 yellow jelly beans

MILDRED MOUSE

2 tablespoons
    desiccated coconut
2 pink Mallow Bakes
1 black licorice strap

PAMELA PANDA

2 tablespoons
    desiccated coconut
1 prune
1 black licorice strap
1 white Fizzer
black glossy decorating gel
1 pink mini M&M

BUMBLE BEE

2 tablespoons
    desiccated coconut
yellow colouring
1 black licorice strap
2 brown mini M&M's
¼ cup (35g) white chocolate
    Melts, melted
white glossy decorating gel

WALLY WOMBAT

2 tablespoons
    desiccated coconut
brown colouring
1 brown and black
    licorice allsort
1 chocolate bullet
1 black licorice strap

RED BACK SPIDER

Turn one patty cake upside
down; trim into spider shape.
Spread all over with some of
the black butter cream. Place
coconut and black colouring
in small plastic bag; rub until
coconut is evenly coloured,
press all over body. Cut licorice
strap into thin strips for legs.
Use toothpick to make holes
in spider's body; poke legs
into holes. Position red
Skittles for red markings on
back; position purple Skittles
for eyes. Use black decorating
gel to dot pupils onto eyes.

TOMMY TORTOISE

Turn one patty cake upside
down; trim into tortoise shape.
Spread all over with some of
the green butter cream. Break
freckles coarsely; press onto
back to form shell. Trim jube;
position for head. Using black
decorating gel, mark eyes
and mouth on head. Press
jelly beans into side for legs.

MILDRED MOUSE

Turn one patty cake upside
down; trim into mouse shape.
Spread all over with some
of the white butter cream,
shaping butter cream to
accentuate the pointy nose.
Press desiccated coconut all
over body. Cut Mallow Bakes
in half horizontally; position
two halves for ears and one
for the nose. Trim licorice strap
for tail, whiskers and eyes.

PAMELA PANDA

Turn one patty cake upside
down; trim into panda shape.
Spread all over with some
of the white butter cream.
Press coconut all over face.
Cut prune in half crossways;
secure to head for ears using
a little butter cream. Cut two
circles from licorice strap for
eye patches; secure using a
little butter cream. Halve
Fizzer; secure to black eye
patches using a little butter
cream. Using black decorating
gel, dot pupils on eyes. Trim
small triangle from licorice for
nose and two thin strips for
mouth; secure using a little
butter cream. Position pink
M&M for mouth.

BUMBLE BEE

Turn one patty cake upside
down; trim into bumble bee
shape. Spread all over with
some of the yellow butter
cream. Place coconut and
yellow colouring in a small
plastic bag; rub until coconut
is evenly coloured, press all
over body. Trim licorice strap
to make stripes and antennae;
secure with a little butter cream.
Secure M&M's for eyes. Draw
two 3cm x 5cm wing outlines
on baking paper. Place melted
chocolate Melts into piping
bag (page 209); pipe chocolate
over tracings. Drizzle extra
chocolate inside outlines to
create wing pattern; refrigerate
until set; push into body of bee.
Using white decorating gel,
pipe dots onto eyes for pupils
and on tips of antennae.

WALLY WOMBAT

Turn one patty cake upside
down; trim into wombat shape.
Spread all over with some of
the brown butter cream. Place
coconut and brown colouring
in small plastic bag; rub until
coconut is evenly coloured,
press all over body. Cut two
triangles from allsort; position
for ears. Cut two slices from
chocolate bullet; position for
eyes. Trim licorice strap to
make nose and feet; secure
using a little butter cream.

funny faces

CAKE

340g packet buttercake mix
1 quantity butter cream (page 206)
yellow, red, green and blue colouring

TIP The buttercake mix and butter
cream are enough to make 12 patty
cakes. Decorate the remaining six
patty cakes with your own favourite
funny faces.

DECORATIONS

(Enough for six patty cakes.)
1 tablespoon apricot jam,
    warmed, sieved
icing sugar mixture
250g ready-made soft icing
flesh colouring
cake decorating stars
cake decorating hearts
cake decorating moons
12 assorted coloured mini M&M's
red glossy decorating gel
black glossy decorating gel

1 Preheat oven to moderate. Line 12-hole
(⅓-cup/80ml) muffin pan with paper
patty cases. Make cake according to
directions on packet, pour ¼ cup mixture
into each hole; bake in moderate oven
about 20 minutes. Stand cakes in pan
5 minutes; turn onto wire rack to cool.

2 Divide butter cream among four small
bowls; tint each with one of the suggested
colours: yellow, red, green and blue.

3 Brush tops of cakes with jam.

4 On surface dusted with icing sugar,
knead soft icing until smooth. Knead
flesh colouring into icing; roll icing until
3mm thick. Using 7.5cm round cutter,
cut six rounds from icing; cover each
patty cake with one round.

5 Place yellow butter cream into piping bag
(page 209) fitted with a fluted tube; pipe
random hairstyles onto one or two patty
cakes. Repeat with red, green and blue
butter creams, cleaning or replacing piping
bag between colours.

6 Decorate hairstyles with stars, hearts and
moons. Position M&M's on each cake for
eyes; secure with tiny dabs of butter cream.

7 Using red and black decorating gels, pipe
pupils, eyebrows, noses, freckles, mouths,
eyelashes, ears and glasses onto cakes.

daisy bunch

CAKE

340g packet buttercake mix
1½ quantities butter cream
   (page 206)
yellow and pink colouring
40cm x 50cm prepared rectangular
   board (page 206)

DECORATIONS

2 x 250g packets coloured
   marshmallows
5 purple Smarties
7 pink Smarties
icing sugar mixture
350g ready-made soft icing
green colouring
pink bow
16 spearmint leaves

1 Preheat oven to moderate. Line 12-hole
   (⅓-cup/80ml) muffin pan with paper
   patty cases. Make cake according to
   directions on packet, pour ¼ cup mixture
   into each hole; bake in moderate oven
   about 20 minutes. Stand cakes in pan
   5 minutes; turn onto wire rack to cool.

2 Tint one-third of the butter cream with
   yellow colouring; spread over five cakes.
   Tint remaining butter cream with pink
   colouring; spread over remaining cakes.

3 Using scissors, cut 18 pink marshmallows
   and 24 yellow marshmallows in half
   horizontally. Squeeze ends of each
   marshmallow together to form petals.
   Decorate pink cakes with six or seven
   yellow marshmallow petals and yellow
   cakes with six or seven pink
   marshmallow petals.

4 Position purple Smarties in centre of pink
   flowers; position pink Smarties in centre
   of yellow flowers. Position flowers on
   prepared board.

5 On surface dusted with icing sugar,
   knead soft icing until smooth. Knead
   green colouring into icing; divide icing
   into quarters. Roll one-quarter of the icing
   into 5mm thick cord. Enclose remaining
   icing in plastic wrap; reserve. Cut icing
   cord into three uneven lengths; position on
   board. Repeat with reserved icing to make
   12 stems in total.

6 Pinch stems together near ends; secure
   bow with a little butter cream. Position
   spearmint leaves along stems; secure
   with a little butter cream.

Using scissors, cut marshmallows in half
then squeeze ends together to form petals.

ball°on bouquet

CAKE

2 x 340g packets buttercake mix
3 quantities butter cream
   (page 206)
red, pink, green, yellow, orange,
   blue and purple colouring
40cm x 60cm prepared rectangular
   board (page 206)

DECORATIONS

white glossy decorating gel
nine 50cm lengths of narrow
   coloured ribbons

1   Preheat oven to moderate. Grease two
    12-hole (⅓-cup/80ml) muffin pans. Make
    cakes according to directions on packets,
    divide mixture evenly among holes in
    muffin pans; bake in moderate oven
    about 20 minutes. Stand cakes in pans
    5 minutes; turn onto wire rack to cool;
    trim cakes, if necessary.

2   Divide butter cream among seven small
    bowls. Tint butter cream red, pink, green,
    yellow, orange, blue and purple.

3   Insert fork into base of each cake to act
    as a handle. Spread tops and sides of
    cakes with butter cream; remove fork
    and arrange balloons on prepared board.

4   Using white decorating gel, pipe a letter
    onto each balloon to spell out appropriate
    birthday message.

5   Using a skewer, tuck ends of coloured
    ribbon under some of the balloons.

Insert fork into base of each cake; spread
tops and sides with butter cream.

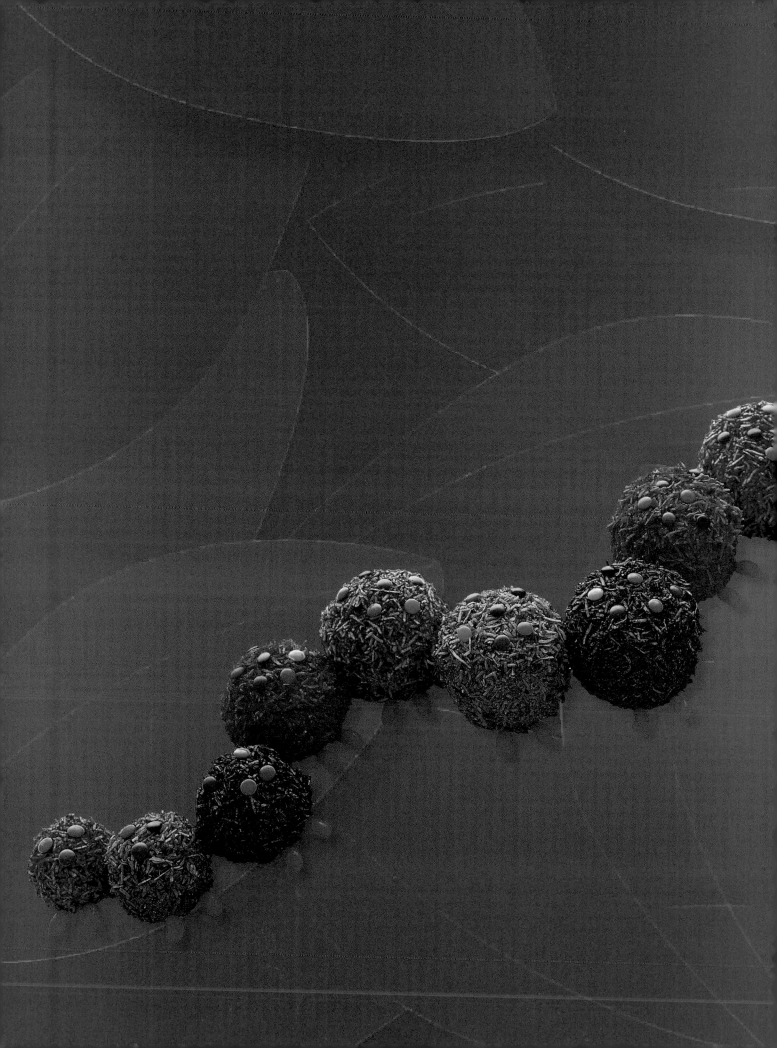

colin caterpillar

CAKE

2 x 340g packets buttercake mix
2 quantities butter cream
　　(page 206)
orange, red, green and
　　blue colouring
4 cups (280g) shredded coconut
45cm x 80cm prepared rectangular
　　board (page 206)

DECORATIONS

44 yellow jelly beans
2 brown Smarties
2 large round mints
1 black licorice strap
1 pink Fruit Stick or Musk Stick
1 yellow Fruit Stick
1 green Fruit Stick
2 yellow chenille sticks
　　(pipe cleaners)
59 mini M&M's

4 Spread each coloured butter cream over tops and sides of three cakes.

5 Place 1 cup coconut and orange colouring in a small plastic bag; rub until coconut is evenly coloured, gently press onto same coloured cake. Repeat with remaining coconut, colouring and cakes.

6 Assemble coconut-covered cakes on prepared board to form caterpillar. Position jelly beans as feet.

7 Using a little butter cream, attach Smarties to mints for eyes; position on cake. Cut licorice strap into thin strip; position on cake for mouth.

8 Thinly slice Fruit Sticks lengthways; position on cake for hair. Curl ends of chenille sticks, position on head for antennae. Scatter M&M's over top of remaining cakes.

TIP You will need to buy a 200g packet jelly beans and a 35g tube mini M&M's for this cake.

Trim four of the cakes, making each one slightly smaller than the previous one.

1 Preheat oven to moderate. Grease two 6-hole texas (¾-cup/180ml) muffin pans. Make cakes according to directions on packets, divide mixture evenly among prepared holes; bake in moderate oven about 30 minutes. Stand cakes in pans 5 minutes; turn onto wire racks to cool. Trim cakes, if necessary.

2 Using small knife, trim four of the cakes for the end of the caterpillar's body, making each one slightly smaller than the previous one.

3 Divide butter cream among four bowls; tint each with one of the suggested colours: orange, red, green and blue.

humpty dumpty

CAKE

340g packet
  buttercake mix
1 quantity butter
  cream (page 206)
green and brown
  colouring
30cm x 40cm prepared
  board (page 206)

DECORATIONS

2 x 300g packets
  chocolate-covered
  fruit and nuts
2 tablespoons
  desiccated coconut

HUMPTY DUMPTY

30cm x 4cm-wide tartan ribbon
craft glue
1 Pavlova Magic egg-shaped
  plastic container
35cm x 2cm-wide white ribbon
black and white threads
12cm x 4mm-wide black ribbon
sewing needles
cottonwool
permanent black marker
1 black licorice strap

*It's best to make Humpty Dumpty
several days ahead to allow the glue to
thoroughly dry; alternatively, you could
use a purchased Humpty Dumpty toy.*

1 Preheat oven to moderate. Grease and
  line (page 204) 14cm x 21cm loaf pan.
  Make cake according to directions on
  packet, pour into pan; bake in moderate
  oven about 50 minutes. Stand cake in pan
  5 minutes; turn onto wire rack to cool.
  Using serrated knife, level cake top.

2 Tint one-third of the butter cream with
  green colouring. Spread green butter cream
  into a rough 20cm x 30cm rectangle on
  prepared board.

3 Position cake on butter cream, cut-side
  down. Tint remaining butter cream with
  brown colouring, spread all over cake.

4 Position chocolate-covered fruit and
  nuts over cake.

5 Place coconut and green colouring in
  small plastic bag; rub until coconut is
  evenly coloured. Sprinkle around cake.

6 Position Humpty Dumpty on cake.

HOW TO MAKE
HUMPTY DUMPTY

1 Cut tartan ribbon into two 5cm pieces
  and two 7cm pieces. Using glue, stick
  remaining tartan ribbon around lower
  half of plastic egg container.

2 Cut white ribbon into two 6cm pieces
  and one 23cm piece. Using glue, stick the
  23cm piece of white ribbon above tartan
  ribbon. Fold ends over to form the collar.
  To help hold collar in place while glue is
  drying, wrap a piece of black thread several
  times around white ribbon, as shown. Once
  glue has dried, remove thread.

3 Tie black ribbon into a small bow; glue
  in position.

4 To make hands: Fold the two remaining
  white ribbon pieces in half crossways, sew
  two long ends together. Using a wooden
  skewer, push a little of the cottonwool
  into cavity. Wrap a piece of white thread,
  about 2cm from folded edge, to form wrist.
  Using white thread, sew along folded edge
  to form fingers, as shown.

5 To make arms: Fold the two 5cm tartan
  pieces in half lengthways. Sew long edge
  of each tartan piece together to form a
  tube. Slip one of the hands into the end of
  each tube, secure into place by inserting
  the needle and wrapping black thread
  around the wrist, as shown.

6 Using a wooden skewer stuff arms with a
  little of the cottonwool, as shown. Secure
  ends by sewing 1cm from open ends.

7 To make legs: Fold the 7cm pieces of
  tartan in half lengthways. Sew long edge
  and one short edge of each tartan piece
  together. Using a wooden skewer stuff
  the legs with a little of the cottonwool.
  Bend the sewn short end to make foot;
  stitch in place, as shown. Secure ends
  by sewing 1cm from open ends.

8 Glue arms and legs to body; allow glue
  to dry.

9 Using permanent marker, draw face.

10 Secure licorice on head for hair with a
  little glue.

1

Help secure collar in place with sewing thread.

2

Sew along folded edge with white thread to form fingers.

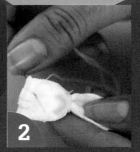

3

Sew tartan edges together to form a tube for the arm.

4

Secure hand to tartan tube by wrapping thread around wrist.

5

Use wooden skewer to gently stuff arm with cottonwool.

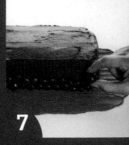

6

Bend end of tartan leg to make a foot, then stitch in place.

7

Position the chocolate-covered fruit and nuts on cake for wall.

8

Sprinkle the green-coloured coconut onto butter cream.

palace of dreams

CAKE

4 x 340g packets buttercake mix
36cm x 46cm prepared rectangular
   board (page 206)
2 x 400g jam rolls
250g packet jam rollettes
bamboo skewers
6 quantities butter cream (page 206)
purple, green and pink colouring
2 Sherbert Cones, filling removed

DECORATIONS

¼ cup (60g) coloured sprinkles
2 teaspoons vegetable oil
250g white chocolate Melts,
   melted
pink, purple and green colouring
60 Sherbet Fizzes or Kool Fruits
10 blue boiled lollies
4 coloured Fruit Sticks
7 coloured marshmallows
assorted mini fairies and frog

This cake is not difficult – it is, however, time consuming.

1 Preheat oven to moderate. Grease and line (page 204) deep 19cm-square cake pan and deep 26cm x 36cm baking dish. Make cakes according to directions on packets, pour a quarter of the mixture into square pan and remaining mixture into baking dish; bake square cake in moderate oven about 35 minutes and cake in baking dish about 1 hour. Stand cakes 10 minutes; turn onto wire racks to cool. Using serrated knife, level cake tops.

2 Place large cake on prepared board, cut-side down. Cut three steps for staircase from one short side of cake. Place square cake on bench, cut-side down; cut 4cm x 6cm piece out of one corner. Cut three steps into this piece. Position square cake on top of large cake so cut-out section is at the back of cake; position stairs on large cake.

3 Position jam rolls and rollettes for towers; position tallest tower where square cake was cut. Using small serrated knife, shape tops of three towers. Secure towers with skewers.

4 Tint half the butter cream purple, two-thirds of the remaining butter cream green and the remaining butter cream pink.

5 Place one-third of the purple butter cream in small bowl, tint a deeper purple; spread over stairs and top of square cake. Spread centre tower with pink butter cream. Spread remaining purple butter cream over remaining towers, Sherbet Cones and sides of square cake. Roll Sherbet Cones in half the coloured sprinkles; position on front towers. Spread green butter cream over top and sides of large cake.

6 Stir oil into melted chocolate; tint two-fifths of the chocolate pink. Spread over baking paper; stand until almost set. Cut chocolate into 1.5cm x 2cm tiles. Position tiles on roofs of two towers. Cut two tiles into pointed pieces; position for spires.

7 Tint two-thirds of remaining melted chocolate purple. Using half the purple chocolate, spread over baking paper; stand until almost set, then cut into 1.5cm x 2cm tiles and a spire; position on third tower. Reserve remaining purple chocolate.

8 Draw three 2.5cm x 3cm windows, one 3cm x 4cm window, two 1.5cm x 4cm window shutters and two 5cm x 10cm gates on baking paper. Turn paper over so outlines are underneath. Spoon reserved purple chocolate into piping bag (page 209), pipe over tracings; stand until set.

9 Tint remaining melted chocolate green, spoon into piping bag; pipe vines on gates and a few smaller vines on baking paper, stand until set.

10 Position windows, window shutters, gates and vines on castle; use Sherbet Fizzes to outline garden. Place boiled lollies in plastic bag; use rolling pin or meat mallet to crush coarsely. Use for ponds.

11 Make mushrooms using Fruit Sticks for stems and marshmallows for caps; place mushrooms around castle. Brush tops of mushrooms with a little water; sprinkle lightly with some of the coloured sprinkles.

12 Scatter more coloured sprinkles around castle. Position fairies and frog on cake.

TIP Be sure to remove skewers before cutting and serving cake.

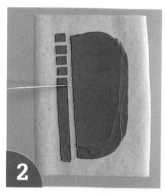

Assemble cakes, jam rolls, rollettes and staircase to make castle.

Spread pink chocolate onto baking paper; when almost set, cut into tiles.

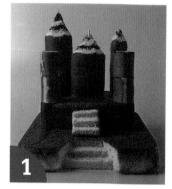

Overlap chocolate tiles to cover roofs of towers; use pointed piece for each spire.

4

Use purple chocolate to pipe windows and window shutters onto baking paper.

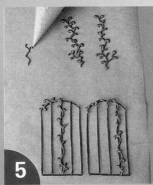

5

Use coloured chocolate to pipe gates and vines onto baking paper.

princess shazza

CAKE

2 x 340g packets buttercake mix
40cm-round prepared board
 (page 206)
1 quantity butter cream (page 206)

DECORATIONS

28cm-tall doll, legs removed
15 white marshmallows
54 pink marshmallows
65 small artificial craft flowers
40cm white ribbon
40cm purple ribbon
1 elastic band
10-piece purple craft feathers

1 Preheat oven to moderate. Grease
 2.5-litre (10-cup) Dolly Varden pan.
 Make cake according to directions on
 packets, pour mixture into prepared pan;
 bake in moderate oven about 1 hour.
 Stand cake in pan 5 minutes; turn onto
 wire rack to cool. Using serrated knife,
 level cake top.

2 Position cake on prepared board, cut-side
 down. Using a teaspoon, scoop a hole
 from top of cake deep enough to fit doll.

3 Spread butter cream all over cake.

4 Cut white marshmallows in half vertically;
 press around base of skirt. Cut pink
 marshmallows in half horizontally;
 gently press all over skirt starting
 from the base, as shown.

5 Position remaining white marshmallows at
 top of skirt. Press artificial flowers randomly
 on skirt between marshmallows.

6 Wind white ribbon around doll's body to
 make halter-top; tie at back. Wind purple
 ribbon around waist. Tie up hair with
 elastic band; push in feather piece and
 artificial flower.

7 Gently push doll into cake to waist level.

TIPS We used a stem of small plastic
flowers, available from craft shops.
If using silk flowers, position on cake
just before serving to prevent butter
cream absorbing into the flowers and
looking greasy.

You need 2 x 250g packets marshmallows
for this recipe.

Position marshmallows on cake.

Press flowers into the cake.

Push doll into hole in top of cake.

the magic toadstool

CAKE

2 x 340g packets buttercake mix
35cm x 50cm prepared rectangular
   board (page 206)
1½ quantities butter cream
   (page 206)
yellow and pink colouring
15cm-round cardboard

DECORATIONS

4 pink Fruit Sticks or Musk Sticks
2 spearmint leaves
8 mini heart lollies
1 yellow Fruit Stick
25 large heart lollies
24 silver cachous
3 large white marshmallows
3 white marshmallows
1 teaspoon cocoa powder
assorted tiny fairies

1 Preheat oven to moderate; grease
1.25-litre (5-cup) and 2.25-litre (9-cup)
pudding steamers. Make cakes according
to directions on packets, pour mixture
into steamers until three-quarters full;
bake smaller pudding in moderate oven
about 35 minutes and larger pudding
about 55 minutes. Stand cakes in steamers
5 minutes; turn onto wire rack to cool.
Using serrated knife, level cake tops.

2 Place small cake on prepared board,
cut-side down. Tint half the butter
cream with yellow colouring; spread
all over cake for toadstool stem.

3 Place large cake on cardboard round,
cut-side down. Position large cake on
toadstool stem for toadstool cap. Tint
remaining butter cream with pink
colouring; spread all over cap.

4 Place pink Fruit Sticks, side by side, on
flat surface; trim tops of sticks to make
rounded door. Position on toadstool stem
for door.

5 Split spearmint leaves in half horizontally;
slice halves into three pieces, as shown.
Use centre pieces for stems and side pieces
as leaves; position around toadstool stem.
Position two mini heart lollies at top of
each spearmint stem for flowers.

6 Cut yellow Fruit Stick into thin strips;
using a little water, position on two large
heart lollies; position on toadstool stem
for windows.

7 Position six large heart lollies on board
at front of toadstool for path. Decorate
toadstool cap with cachous and
remaining large heart lollies.

8 Using a little butter cream, attach
large marshmallows on top of smaller
marshmallows, sprinkle with sifted cocoa;
position around toadstool. Position fairies
around toadstool.

TIPS You can make patty cakes with
any leftover cake mixture.

If you can't find large hearts, use love
hearts, the ones with messages on them,
instead. Just turn them word-side down.

Position large cake on small cake,
then spread pink butter cream
over toadstool cap.

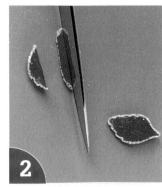

Split spearmint leaves in half
through centre then slice the
halves into three pieces.

island girl

CAKE

2 x 340g packets buttercake mix
40cm-round prepared board
   (page 206)
⅓ cup (110g) apricot jam,
   warmed, sieved

DECORATIONS

icing sugar mixture
750g ready-made soft icing
green colouring
28cm-tall doll, legs removed
1 egg white
14 sour apple karate belts
small string artificial craft flowers

1 Preheat oven to moderate. Grease
2.5-litre (10-cup) Dolly Varden pan.
Make cake according to directions on
packets, pour mixture into prepared pan;
bake in moderate oven about 1 hour.
Stand cake in pan 5 minutes; turn onto
wire rack to cool. Using serrated knife,
level cake top.

2 Place cake on prepared board, cut-side
down. Brush cake with jam.

3 On surface lightly dusted with sifted icing
sugar, knead soft icing until smooth.
Knead green colouring into icing; roll
icing until 5mm thick. Using rolling pin,
carefully lift icing over cake. Using hands
dusted with icing sugar, mould icing to
completely cover cake; rub icing gently
with hands to smooth. Trim excess icing
away from base.

4 Cut small hole in top of cake deep
enough to fit doll.

5 Brush top third of the cake with
egg white. Slice karate belts in half
lengthways. Position karate belts
over cake to resemble grass skirt.

6 Gently push doll into cake to waist level.

7 Thread flowers onto piece of string to
create lei. Position around doll's neck.
Place flower in doll's hair.

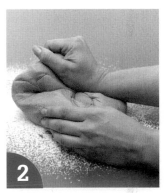
Brush cake with warmed jam.

Knead green colouring into icing.

Mould icing onto cake.

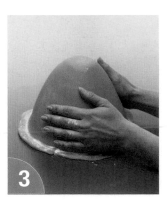
Trim excess icing from cake.

gary ghost

ghost

CAKE

340g packet buttercake mix
30cm x 40cm prepared rectangular
  board (page 206)
1 quantity fluffy frosting (page 208)

DECORATIONS

red permanent marker
1 egg shell, halved
2 red Smarties
12 blue Smarties

1 Preheat oven to moderate. Grease and line (page 204) 19cm x 29cm rectangular slice pan. Make cake according to directions on packet, pour into pan; bake in moderate oven about 25 minutes. Stand cake in pan 5 minutes; turn onto wire rack to cool. Using serrated knife, level cake top.

2 Turn cake, cut-side down. Cut two corners off cake, as shown.

3 Position cake on prepared board, cut-side down; position corners for ghost's arms, as shown.

4 Using permanent marker, draw veins in egg shells. Use a little frosting to secure red Smarties in egg shells for eyes.

5 Spread fluffy frosting all over cake. Position egg shells for eyes and blue Smarties for mouth.

TIP Rinse egg shells with cold water; leave to dry.

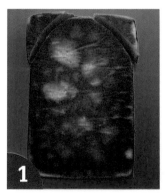

Cut corners off the cake.

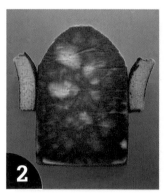

Assemble cake on board.

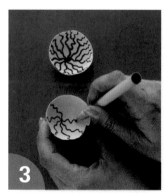

Draw veins in egg shells.

girlie ghost

CAKE

2 x 340g packets buttercake mix
40cm-round prepared board
    (page 206)
1 quantity butter cream (page 206)
blue colouring

DECORATIONS

icing sugar mixture
1.2kg ready-made soft icing
purple bow

1 Preheat oven to moderate. Grease 2.5-litre
   (10-cup) Dolly Varden pan. Make cake
   according to directions on packets, pour
   mixture into pan; bake in moderate oven
   about 1 hour. Stand cake in pan 5 minutes;
   turn onto wire rack to cool. Using serrated
   knife, level cake top.

2 Place cake on board, cut-side down. Tint
   butter cream with blue colouring; spread
   all over cake.

3 On surface dusted with icing sugar,
   knead soft icing until smooth; roll icing
   into 5mm-thick circle large enough to
   generously cover cake. Using metal
   cutters or small sharp-pointed knife,
   cut eyes and mouth near centre of icing
   circle. Using rolling pin, lift icing over
   cake, draping so the cut-out eyes and
   mouth are positioned in the right place.
   (Icing will stretch slightly when lifted over
   the cake.) Trim draped icing on board to
   neaten shape of ghost.

4 Using a little butter cream, secure bow
   to cake.

Tint the butter cream with blue
colouring then, using a palette
knife, spread it all over the cake.

Using a metal circular cutter and
tear-shaped cutter, cut eyes and
mouth from the icing.

the good witch

CAKE

2 x 340g packets buttercake mix
40cm x 50cm prepared rectangular
  board (page 206)
1 quantity butter cream (page 206)
blue and purple colouring

DECORATIONS

1 black licorice strap
4 licorice allsorts
1 packet potato straws
2 pink Fizzers
1 black licorice twist

1 Preheat oven to moderate. Grease and
   line (page 204) 20cm x 30cm lamington
   pan. Make cake according to directions
   on packets, pour into pan; bake in
   moderate oven about 40 minutes. Stand
   cake in pan 5 minutes; turn onto wire
   rack to cool. Using serrated knife, level
   cake top.

2 Turn cake cut-side down. Using paper
   pattern from pattern sheet, cut witch
   from cake. Place cake on prepared board,
   cut-side down; discard remaining cake.

3 Tint ½ cup butter cream with blue
   colouring. Tint remaining butter cream
   with purple colouring. Spread purple
   butter cream all over cake; spread blue
   butter cream over face and hands.

4 Cut licorice strap into thin strips; position
   on cake for hat outline, tassel, dress and
   face. Cut stars out of licorice allsorts;
   position on witch's dress. Position potato
   straws for hair and pink Fizzers for eyes.

5 Cut licorice twist in half; position on
   either side of witch. Position thin licorice
   strips for bristles; wind thin licorice around
   join between bristles and broom handle.

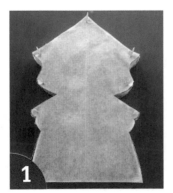

Cut out cake using paper pattern.

Cut stars from licorice allsorts.

Fantasy

villainous vampire

CAKE

2 x 340g packets buttercake mix
33cm x 41cm prepared rectangular
   board (page 206)
2 quantities butter cream (page 206)
black, red and brown colouring

DECORATIONS

1 black licorice strap
1 large teeth lolly
2 milk bottles
2 black Smarties
1 red bow

1 Preheat oven to moderate. Grease and line (page 204) deep 32cm-long oval cake tin. Make cake according to directions on packets, pour into pan; bake in moderate oven about 40 minutes. Stand cake in pan 10 minutes; turn onto wire rack to cool. Using serrated knife, level cake top.

2 Turn cake cut-side down. Using paper pattern from pattern sheet, cut vampire from cake. Place cake on prepared board, cut-side down; discard remaining cake.

3 Using toothpick or fine shewer, mark features onto cake.

4 Spread 1 cup of butter cream evenly over face and ears. Tint 1½ cups of remaining butter cream black; reserve 2 tablespoons. Spread black butter cream over hair and collar. Tint ½ cup of remaining butter cream red. Spoon small amount into piping bag (page 209); pipe bloodshot lines for eyes. Spread lips and blood droplets with remaining red butter cream.

5 Tint remaining cream pale brown, use to pipe facial lines. Pipe reserved black butter cream around eyes; fill in nostrils and mouth.

6 Cut eyebrows from licorice strap, position on cake. Position teeth on cake; cut milk bottles in half vertically, position on cake.

7 Position Smarties on cake for eyes. Position bow under vampire's chin.

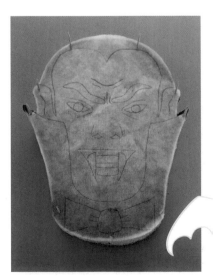

Attach pattern to cake using toothpicks before cutting out cake.

wicked Wizard's hat

CAKE

3 x 340g packets buttercake mix
43cm x 47cm prepared rectangular
   board (page 206)
2 quantities butter cream (page 206)
blue colouring

DECORATIONS

silver cardboard, for buckle
1 black licorice strap
100g white chocolate Melts,
   melted
yellow colouring
coloured sprinkles

1 Preheat oven to moderate. Grease
   and line (page 204) deep 26cm x 36cm
   baking dish. Make cake according to
   directions on packets, pour into dish;
   bake in moderate oven about 1 hour.
   Stand cake in dish 10 minutes; turn
   onto wire rack to cool. Using serrated
   knife, level cake top.

2 Turn cake cut-side down. Using paper
   pattern from pattern sheet, cut hat
   from cake.

3 Assemble cake on prepared board, cut-side
   down, to form hat; discard remaining cake.

4 Tint butter cream with blue colouring;
   spread all over cake.

5 Trace buckle shape (see outline, page 55);
   copy onto silver cardboard, then cut out
   shape. Weave licorice strap through
   buckle; position on cake.

6 Trace stars (see outline, page 55) onto
   baking paper. Turn paper over so outlines
   are underneath. Combine melted chocolate
   and yellow colouring in small bowl. Spoon
   into piping bag (page 209); pipe over
   tracings of stars. Top half the stars with
   coloured sprinkles; stand until set.
   Carefully lift stars from baking paper;
   position on cake.

TIP You also can use star-patterned
wrapping paper, with a sheet of baking
paper over it, as a guide when tracing
the stars.

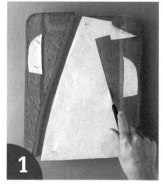

Use paper pattern to cut wizard's
hat from cake.

Spread butter cream over cake
using palette knife.

Pipe stars; sprinkle half with
coloured sprinkles.

BUCKLE   STAR

*jo*e bad

CAKE

3 x 340g packets buttercake mix
30cm x 41cm prepared rectangular
 board (page 206)
toothpicks
2 quantities butter cream (page 206)
pink, black, purple, yellow, blue,
 red, green and orange colouring

DECORATIONS

1 black licorice strap
2 safety pins

1 Preheat oven to moderate. Grease
   and line (page 204) two 20cm x 30cm
   lamington pans. Make cakes according
   to directions on packets, divide mixture
   between pans; bake in moderate oven
   about 35 minutes. Stand cakes in pans
   5 minutes; turn onto wire racks to cool.
   Using serrated knife, level cake tops so
   they are the same height.

2 Turn cakes cut-side down. Using paper
   pattern from pattern sheet, cut out Joe
   from cake; place Joe on prepared board,
   cut-side down; discard remaining cake.

3 Using toothpick or fine skewer, mark Joe's
   outlines onto cake.

4 Tint half the butter cream with pink
   colouring, reserve 2 tablespoons. Spread
   face, except mouth, glasses and hair, with
   pink butter cream.

5 Divide remaining butter cream into seven
   equal portions; colour each portion with
   one of the remaining colours.

6 Make sunglasses with some of the black
   butter cream; create lips with some of the
   purple butter cream.

7 Tint reserved pink butter cream a darker
   pink. Spoon into piping bag (page 209);
   pipe outlines for nose, ears and jaw.

8 Make spiked hair with different coloured
   butter creams. Run a toothpick through
   hair to create texture.

9 Mark hairline and stubble using a bunch
   of toothpicks dipped into black colouring.

10 Position licorice strap for sunglasses strap.
   Position safety pins.

   TIP Ensure the safety pins are removed
   before serving cake.

Assemble cakes then, using paper
pattern, cut out cake.

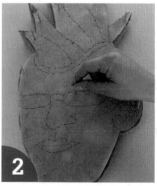

Use a toothpick to mark out Joe's
features on cake.

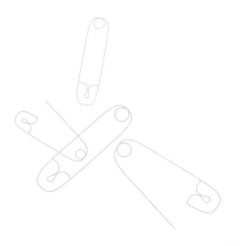

To make facial stubble, use toothpicks
dipped in black colouring.

castle of darkness

CAKE

3 x 340g packets buttercake mix
30cm-round prepared board
  (page 206)
2 quantities butter cream (page 206)
blue colouring
2 jam rollettes

DECORATIONS

1 bamboo skewer
8cm-round black cardboard
6 chocolate mint sticks
150g white chocolate Melts,
  melted
yellow colouring
100g milk chocolate Melts, melted
27 sections dark chocolate
  Toblerone
artificial spider's web

Place one 20cm cake on prepared board then spread the cut side with ½ cup of butter cream.

1 Preheat oven to moderate. Grease and line (page 204) deep 13cm-round cake pan and two deep 20cm-round cake pans. Make cakes according to directions on packets, pour mixture into 13cm pan until three-quarters full. Divide remaining mixture between 20cm pans; bake 13cm cake in moderate oven about 35 minutes and 20cm cakes about 40 minutes. Stand cakes in pans 5 minutes; turn onto wire racks to cool. Using serrated knife, level cake tops.

2 Place one 20cm cake on board, cut-side up. Tint butter cream with blue colouring; spread cake top with ½ cup of the butter cream. Top cake with remaining 20cm cake, cut-side down. Spread cut-side of 13cm cake with ¼ cup of butter cream; centre, butter-cream down, on 20cm cake stack.

3 Position rollettes on top of stacked cakes; secure with skewer, as shown. Spread remaining butter cream all over cakes.

4 Cut slit from edge to centre of black cardboard; roll cardboard into cone shape, as shown. Secure with sticky tape on inside of cone; position cone on cake top.

5 Position mint sticks together on bottom of cake for door.

6 Draw five 3cm x 5.5cm and seven 2cm x 3cm windows on sheet of baking paper. Turn paper over so outlines are underneath. Tint white chocolate with yellow colouring; place in piping bag (page 209). Pipe windows onto baking paper; stand until chocolate sets.

7 Place milk chocolate in separate piping bag. Pipe spiders onto sheet of baking paper; stand until chocolate sets.

8 Decorate castle with windows, spiders, Toblerone and spider's web.

TIPS You can find artificial spider's web at novelty shops. If you can't find it, use fairy floss or cottonwool, instead. Be sure to remove spider's web or cottonwool before cutting and serving cake.

You will need approximately 3 x 100g bars of Toblerone for this recipe.

Stack the jam rollettes on the cake then secure them with a skewer to make a tower.

Cut a small slit from the edge to centre of the black cardboard, then roll it to form a cone.

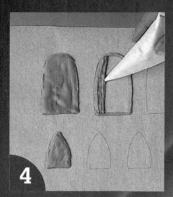

4

Pipe different-sized windows onto a sheet of baking paper; stand until set.

5

Using milk chocolate, pipe spiders onto a sheet of baking paper; stand until set.

zappo the alien

CAKE

2 x 340g packets buttercake mix
30cm x 46cm prepared rectangular
board (page 206)
2 quantities butter cream (page 206)
green colouring

DECORATIONS

2 yellow Skittles
2 giant Jaffas
27 green Skittles
1 red fruit ring
rainbow choc-chips
2 green lollipops
7 spearmint leaves
7 toothpicks
21 orange and yellow Kool Fruits

1 Preheat oven to moderate; grease and line (page 204) deep 20cm-round cake pan and deep 18cm-oval cake pan. Make cakes according to directions on packets; divide mixture between pans so that both mixtures are the same depth. Bake round cake in moderate oven about 35 minutes and oval cake about 40 minutes. Stand cakes in pans 5 minutes; turn onto wire racks to cool.

2 Assemble cakes on prepared board, top-side up, as shown.

3 Tint butter cream with green colouring; use a little butter cream to attach oval cake to round cake. Spread remaining butter cream all over cakes.

4 Attach yellow Skittles to Jaffas with a little butter cream for eyes; position on cake. Position one green Skittle for nose; position fruit ring for mouth. Sprinkle rainbow choc-chips on cheeks and top of head; position lollipops on head for antennae.

5 Skewer each spearmint leaf with a toothpick; position on sides and top of head. Position Kool Fruits and remaining green Skittles on body of alien.

TIPS You will need one 200g packet of Skittles for this cake and one 120g packet of Kool Fruits.

Be sure to remove toothpicks from cake before cutting and serving.

Assemble cooled cakes on prepared board, top-side up.

Spread green butter cream all over top and sides of cakes.

psycho-deliah

CAKE

3 x 340g packets buttercake mix
½ cup (160g) apricot jam,
    warmed, sieved
30cm-round prepared board
    (page 206)

DECORATIONS

icing sugar mixture
1.5kg ready-made soft icing
flesh and red colouring
1 black licorice rope
100 wooden toothpicks,
    with double-pointed ends
4 x 200g packets Psychedelic
    Snakes Alive
1 large teeth lolly
2 green jubes
2 purple Smarties
2 mini red M&M's
26 silver cachous
1 black licorice strap
2 blue cachous

Brush cut-side of each cake with a little jam; join the cut-sides to make a head.

Using hands dusted with icing sugar, rub icing to cover head and make smooth.

Insert a toothpick into each snake then press into head for hair.

1 Preheat oven to moderate. Grease two 1.75-litre (7-cup) pudding steamers. Make cakes according to directions on packets, divide mixture between steamers; bake in moderate oven about 50 minutes. Stand cakes in steamers 5 minutes; turn onto wire racks to cool. Using serrated knife, level cake tops.

2 Brush cut-side of cakes with some of the jam; join cut-sides together to make head. Position head on board; brush with remaining jam.

3 On surface dusted with icing sugar, knead soft icing until smooth. Knead flesh colouring into icing; roll 1.25kg of the icing until 5mm thick, enclose remaining icing in plastic wrap. Using rolling pin, carefully lift icing onto cake. Using hands dusted with icing sugar, mould icing to completely cover head; rub icing gently with hands to smooth.

4 Trim licorice rope for collar to fit around base of head; secure collar to the head with toothpick.

5 Insert toothpick into one end of each snake; press into head for hair. Cut snakes in half at front for fringe.

6 Place about 1 teaspoon of reserved icing in a cup; stir in a drop or two of warm water to make a thick paste. Cover paste; reserve.

7 Using hands dusted with icing sugar, shape remaining icing into eyebrows and lips. Trim gum of teeth lolly to fit into lips. Dab a little of the reserved paste onto the back of the mouth and eyebrows; position on head.

8 Using paste, position one jube on face for nose, Smarties under brows for eyes and M&M's on Smarties for pupils.

9 Cut remaining jube into small triangles; position on face with paste for eyelashes.

10 Using paste, attach silver cachous to collar. Cut small piece from licorice strap for eyebrow ring; position on cake. Using paste, attach one blue cachous on eyebrow ring. Using paste, attach blue cachous to nose for nose stud. Using red colouring and small paintbrush, paint eyebrows and lips, then freckles on cheeks.

TIPS Be sure to remove all toothpicks from cake before cutting and serving.

If you can't find Psychedelic Snakes Alive, you can use 4 x 225g packets of Snakes Alive, instead.

4 Shape the remaining icing into eyebrows and lips, then place the teeth lolly in position.

5 Cut remaining green jube into small triangles, then position on face for eyelashes.

prOwling tigers

CAKE

340g packet buttercake mix
30cm-round prepared board
   (page 206)
1 quantity butter cream (page 206)
yellow colouring

DECORATIONS

1 tablespoon blue jelly crystals
⅓ cup (80ml) boiling water
2 x 200g packets chocolate finger
   biscuits
¼ cup (20g) desiccated coconut,
   toasted
1 spearmint leaf
30g Flake, halved
6 small chocolate-covered nuts
2 toy tigers
2 teaspoons desiccated
   coconut, extra
green colouring

1 Preheat oven to moderate. Grease and
   line (page 204) deep 22cm-round cake
   pan. Make cake according to directions on
   packet, pour into pan; bake in moderate
   oven about 30 minutes. Stand cake in
   pan 5 minutes; turn onto wire rack to
   cool. Using serrated knife, level cake top.

2 Combine jelly and the boiling water in
   small jug; stir until jelly crystals dissolve,
   refrigerate until almost set.

3 Place cake on prepared board, cut-side
   down. Using small knife, cut small pond
   shape in top of cake.

4 Tint butter cream with yellow colouring,
   spread all over cake.

5 Position chocolate fingers around side
   of cake. Sprinkle toasted coconut over
   cake, avoiding pond.

6 When jelly is almost set, stir gently;
   spoon into hollowed section of cake.
   Cut spearmint leaf into thin curvy
   strips, place on side of pond.

7 Position Flake, nuts and tigers on cake.

8 Place extra coconut and green colouring
   in small plastic bag; rub until coconut is
   evenly coloured. Sprinkle green coconut
   in various places on cake.

pony club

CAKE

340g packet buttercake mix
30cm-round prepared board
   (page 206)
1 quantity butter cream (page 206)
green colouring

DECORATIONS

2 x 200g packets chocolate finger
   biscuits
½ cup (45g) desiccated coconut
green colouring
2 tablespoons shredded coconut
2 toy horses
2 toy riders
1 tablespoon shredded coconut,
   extra, toasted

1 Preheat oven to moderate. Grease and
   line (page 204) deep 22cm-round cake
   pan. Make cake according to directions on
   packet, pour into pan; bake in moderate
   oven about 30 minutes. Stand cake in
   pan 5 minutes; turn onto wire rack to
   cool. Using serrated knife, level cake top.

2 Place cake on prepared board, cut-side
   down.

3 Tint butter cream with green colouring,
   spread all over cake.

4 Position one chocolate finger along base
   of cake, position one finger diagonally.
   Cut another finger in half and position to
   make gate. Position remaining chocolate
   fingers around side of cake.

5 Place desiccated coconut and green
   colouring in small plastic bag; rub
   until coconut is evenly coloured.
   Sprinkle over cake.

6 Place shredded coconut and green
   colouring in small plastic bag; rub
   until coconut is evenly coloured.
   Sprinkle around top edge of cake.
   Position horses and dolls on cake.
   Sprinkle toasted coconut in front of
   one horse.

teddy bears' picnic

CAKE

340g packet buttercake mix
30cm-round prepared board
   (page 206)
1 quantity butter cream (page 206)
green colouring

DECORATIONS

10 spearmint leaves
48 mini M&M's
10cm-square piece of fabric
2 small teddy bears
2 small picnic settings
1 small picnic basket with assorted
   foods, drinks and napkins

1   Preheat oven to moderate. Grease and line
    (page 204) deep 20cm-round cake pan.
    Make cake according to directions on
    packet, pour into pan; bake in moderate
    oven about 40 minutes. Stand cake in pan
    5 minutes; turn onto wire rack to cool.
    Using serrated knife, level cake top.

2   Place cake on prepared board, cut-side
    down.

3   Tint butter cream with green colouring.
    Reserve 2 tablespoons of green butter
    cream; tint reserved butter cream slightly
    darker green. Spread light green butter
    cream all over cake. Swirl darker green
    butter cream over top of cake.

4   Cut spearmint leaves into thin strips with
    scissors; position around side of cake to
    resemble flower stems. Position M&M's
    around side of cake to make flowers.

5   Decorate top of cake with fabric for picnic
    rug, teddies, picnic settings, basket and
    assorted food, drinks and napkins.

    TIP You will need to buy a 35g tube
    of mini M&M's for this recipe.

picture perfect

CAKE

2 x 340g packets buttercake mix
35cm-square prepared board
 (page 206)
2 quantities butter cream (page 206)

DECORATIONS

11cm-square photograph,
 laminated
1kg mixed lollies

1 Preheat oven to moderate. Grease and line (page 204) deep 23cm-square cake pan. Make cake according to directions on packets, pour into pan; bake in moderate oven about 1 hour. Stand cake in pan 5 minutes; turn onto wire rack to cool. Using serrated knife, level cake top.

2 Place cake on prepared board, cut-side down.

3 Spread butter cream all over cake.

4 Centre photograph on cake.

5 Scatter mixed lollies all over cake; press lollies gently into butter cream.

TIPS You can use any photographic print you like, but remember to laminate it if you want it to remain after the cake is gone.

Use a selection of your favourite lollies to decorate this cake.

Carefully position photograph in centre of cake.

surfie chick

CAKE

340g packet buttercake mix
30cm-round prepared board
   (page 206)
1 quantity butter cream (page 206)
blue and yellow colouring

DECORATIONS

300g white chocolate Melts,
   melted
royal blue and orange colouring
small shell chocolate moulds
2 tablespoons almond meal
1 small doll
1 cocktail umbrella
1 packet doll's beach accessories

It's important that the chocolate moulds are thoroughly cleaned and dried before using.

1 Preheat oven to moderate. Grease and line (page 204) deep 20cm-round cake pan. Make cake according to directions on packet, pour into pan; bake in moderate oven about 40 minutes. Stand cake in pan 5 minutes; turn onto wire rack to cool.

2 Meanwhile, divide melted chocolate between two small bowls; tint one portion blue and the other portion orange. Pour blue chocolate into half the moulds. Tap moulds gently on bench to remove air bubbles; using palette knife, level chocolate across each shell. Repeat with orange chocolate. Refrigerate moulds about 10 minutes or until chocolate sets. To release shells from mould, place sheet of baking paper slightly larger than mould on tray; holding mould upside down, tap one edge of the mould gently onto baking paper. Refrigerate shells until required.

3 Place cake on prepared board, top-side up.

4 Reserve ¼ cup of butter cream. Tint two-thirds of remaining butter cream with blue colouring; tint remaining one-third butter cream with yellow colouring.

5 Spread yellow butter cream over top of one-third of the cake. Sprinkle almond meal over yellow butter cream to resemble sand.

6 Spread three-quarters of blue butter cream around side of cake and over remaining two-thirds of top of cake in the shape of waves. Spread remaining blue butter cream and plain butter cream over waves to make peaks.

7 Place chocolate shells around side of cake. Position doll, umbrella and beach accessories on sand.

TIP Work quickly while making the chocolate shells, as the chocolate tends to set quickly. You may need to resoften the chocolate in a microwave oven for a couple of seconds, if this happens.

pink & pretty

CAKE

340g packet buttercake mix
30cm-round prepared board
   (page 206)
1 quantity butter cream (page 206)
green and yellow colouring

DECORATIONS

1½ cups (100g) shredded coconut
green, yellow and pink colouring
icing sugar mixture
500g ready-made soft icing
tiny fairy

1   Preheat oven to moderate. Grease and line
    (page 204) deep 20cm-round cake pan.
    Make cake according to directions on
    packet, pour into pan; bake in moderate
    oven about 40 minutes. Stand cake in pan
    5 minutes; turn onto wire rack to cool.
    Using serrated knife, level cake top.

2   Place cake on prepared board, cut-side
    down.

3   Reserve 2 tablespoons of butter cream.
    Tint remaining butter cream with green
    colouring; spread all over cake.

4   Reserve 1 tablespoon of the coconut.
    Place remaining coconut and green
    colouring in small plastic bag; rub until
    coconut is evenly coloured, gently press
    over top and side of cake.

5   On surface dusted with icing sugar,
    knead soft icing until smooth. Knead pink
    colouring into icing; roll until 5mm thick.

6   Using pattern, printed below, cut six
    petals from icing using sharp-pointed
    knife. Position petals on cake.

7   Tint reserved butter cream with yellow
    colouring. Spread yellow butter cream in
    centre of flower. Place reserved coconut
    and yellow colouring in small plastic bag;
    rub until coconut is evenly coloured, gently
    press into centre of flower.

8   Position fairy on flower.

    TIP Lightly dust paper pattern with
    icing sugar while cutting petals to
    prevent it from sticking to icing.

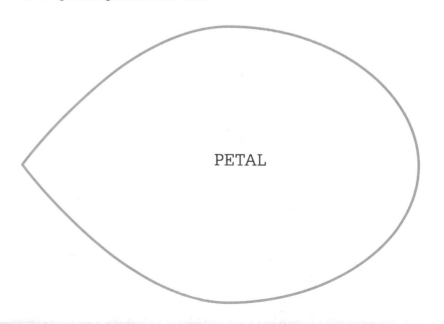

PETAL

under the sea

CAKE

340g packet buttercake mix
30cm-round prepared board
   (page 206)
1 quantity butter cream (page 206)
blue colouring

DECORATIONS

85g packet blue jelly crystals
1 plastic fish
2 chocolate fish
2 plastic monsters
4 jelly sharks
4 jelly snakes
4 jelly small snakes

1 Preheat oven to moderate. Grease and line (page 204) deep 20cm-round cake pan. Make cake according to directions on packet, pour into pan; bake in moderate oven about 40 minutes. Stand cake in pan 5 minutes; turn onto wire rack to cool. Using serrated knife, level cake top.

2 Meanwhile, make jelly according to directions on packet; refrigerate until almost set.

3 Position cake on prepared board, cut-side down. Mark a 15cm circle in centre of cake; cut a hollow into centre of cake about 1cm deep.

4 Tint butter cream with blue colouring; spread all over cake.

5 When jelly is almost set, stir gently; spoon into hollow of cake. Position fish, monsters, sharks and snakes on and around side of cake.

construction site

CAKE

2 x 340g packets buttercake mix
30cm-round prepared board
  (page 206)
2 quantities butter cream (page 206)
yellow colouring

DECORATIONS

2 x 50g Violet Crumble bars, crushed
300g packet chocolate-covered
  fruit and nuts
1 road works sign
1 toy dump truck
2 toy construction workers
2 toy witches' hats

1 Preheat oven to moderate. Grease and line (page 204) deep 22cm-round cake pan. Make cake according to directions on packets, pour into pan; bake in moderate oven about 1 hour. Stand cake in pan 5 minutes; turn onto wire rack to cool.

2 Place cake on prepared board top-side up; using serrated knife, shape cake to make a pit and hill.

3 Tint butter cream with yellow colouring; spread all over cake.

4 Sprinkle cake with Violet Crumble.

5 Place chocolate fruit and nuts around base of cake.

6 Position toys on cake.

TIP Violet Crumbles can be substituted with Crunchie bars or any other chocolate-coated honeycomb.

smiley clock

CAKE

2 x 340g packets buttercake mix
35cm-round prepared board
   (page 206)
2 quantities butter cream (page 206)
yellow colouring

DECORATIONS

250g white chocolate Melts, melted
purple colouring
chocolate number moulds
1 white marshmallow
2 google eyes
1 black licorice strap, cut into
   thin strips
2m x 6mm-wide purple ribbon
120 Smarties

It is important that the chocolate moulds are thoroughly cleaned and dried before using.

1 Preheat oven to moderate. Grease and line (page 204) deep 26cm-round cake pan. Make cake according to directions on packets, pour into pan; bake in moderate oven about 1 hour. Stand cake in pan 5 minutes; turn onto wire rack to cool. Using serrated knife, level cake top.

2 Place cake on prepared board, cut-side down.

3 Meanwhile, tint chocolate with purple colouring. Pour chocolate into number moulds. Tap moulds gently on bench to remove air bubbles; using palette knife, level chocolate across each number. Refrigerate moulds about 10 minutes or until chocolate sets. To release number from mould, place sheet of baking paper slightly larger than mould on tray; holding mould upside down, tap one edge of the mould gently onto baking paper. Repeat process until numbers 1 to 12 have been made.

4 Spread remaining chocolate onto sheet of baking paper; allow to set. Cut two strips of chocolate, 2cm x 5.5cm. Trim edges of one end to a point to form clock hands.

5 Tint butter cream with yellow colouring, reserve 1 tablespoon of the butter cream; spread remaining butter cream all over cake.

6 Arrange chocolate numbers on cake. Split marshmallow in half horizontally. Position marshmallow in centre of cake for nose. Spoon reserved butter cream into piping bag (page 209); pipe around marshmallow.

7 Position chocolate hands on cake. Place eyes in position then arrange licorice on cake for smile and eyelashes.

8 Secure ribbon around cake centre; position Smarties above and below ribbon.

TIPS You will need to buy three 50g packets of Smarties.

Work quickly while making chocolate numbers, as the chocolate tends to set quickly. You may need to resoften the chocolate in a microwave oven for a couple of seconds, if this happens.

sand castle
ice-cream cake

CAKE

3 litres vanilla ice-cream, softened
2 litre plastic sand castle bucket
30cm-round prepared board
  (page 206)

DECORATIONS

1 cup (90g) desiccated coconut
brown and yellow colouring
12 chocolate sea shells
small flag

1 Press ice-cream into clean, dry bucket;
   cover with foil, freeze overnight.

2 Dip base of bucket into hot water for
   a few seconds, invert ice-cream onto
   foil-covered tray; freeze 3 hours.

3 Meanwhile, place coconut, brown and
   yellow colouring in small plastic bag;
   rub colouring into coconut until
   evenly coloured.

4 Transfer ice-cream to prepared board.
   Quickly, press coconut all over cake,
   sprinkle remaining coconut around
   base of cake; freeze until required.

5 Just before serving, arrange chocolate
   sea shells around cake and position flag.

Press the ice-cream into a clean,
dry plastic bucket.

spaceship scorpio

CAKE

2 x 340g packets buttercake mix

40cm x 47cm prepared rectangular
board (page 206)

2 quantities fluffy frosting (page 208)

DECORATIONS

1 black licorice strap

1 green jelly bean

1 sheet gelatine, optional

1 pink marshmallow

1 white marshmallow

5 licorice allsorts, cut in half

6 Smarties

15g packet silver cachous

15g packet gold cachous

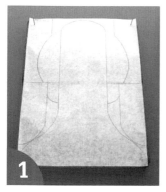

1 Preheat oven to moderate. Grease and line (page 204) two 20cm x 30cm lamington pans. Make cakes according to directions on packets, divide mixture between pans; bake in moderate oven about 30 minutes. Stand cakes in pans 5 minutes; turn onto wire racks to cool. Using serrated knife, level cake tops so cakes are the same height.

2 Turn cakes cut-side down. Using paper pattern from pattern sheet, mark spaceship shape with toothpick or fine skewer. Cut out cake with sharp knife.

3 Assemble cake pieces on prepared board to form spaceship, as shown. Make cockpit from leftover cake; discard remaining cake. Spread fluffy frosting all over cake.

4 Cut licorice strap into thin strips; using licorice, outline spaceship's edges.

5 Position green jelly bean in cockpit to represent space traveller. Cut sheet gelatine to shape of front of cockpit, enclose cockpit with gelatine.

6 Position marshmallows on back of ship to make lights. Position allsorts to make windows and Smarties to make spotlights. Position cachous on top of ship as shown.

Trace pattern onto baking paper; secure on cake with toothpicks.

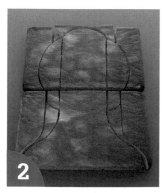

Cut cake, ready to assemble.

Assemble cake to form spaceship shape.

monster
space station

CAKE

2 x 340g packets buttercake mix

3 x 300g packets jam rolls

45cm x 57cm prepared rectangular board (page 206)

2 quantities butter cream (page 206)

green colouring

DECORATIONS

32 Smarties

12 Life Savers

30 mini musks

3 Musk Sticks

8 chocolate mint sticks

3 snowballs

1 Mint Pattie

1 black licorice strap

1 Preheat oven to moderate. Grease and line (page 204) deep 28cm-round cake pan. Make cake according to directions on packets, pour into pan; bake in moderate oven about 45 minutes. Stand cake in pan 10 minutes; turn onto wire rack to cool. Using serrated knife, level cake top.

2 Turn cake cut-side down. Using 12cm-round cutter, cut centre from cake. Using 6cm-round cutter, cut centre from round; discard centre. Cut small ring into three pieces, as shown. Place big ring cake on prepared board, cut-side down.

3 Cut a quarter off one jam roll, position larger piece in hole of cake; discard smaller piece. Cut remaining two jam rolls in half. Position jam rolls at sides and front of space station. Position cut ring pieces, as shown.

4 Tint butter cream with green colouring; spread all over cake.

5 Position Smarties as lights and Life Savers as windows, as shown. Position mini musks on cake.

6 Cut Musk Sticks and three mint sticks in half; position on cake, as shown. Cut remaining mint sticks into 2cm pieces, position on cake as lights.

7 Position snowballs and Mint Pattie on cake.

8 Cut licorice into thin strips; use to outline shape of space station.

Use 12cm cutter to cut centre from cake; use 6cm cutter to cut centre from round.

Cut small ring into three pieces.

Assemble cake to form space station.

rocket blast

CAKE

3 x 340g packets buttercake mix

35cm x 45cm prepared rectangular board (page 206)

2 quantities butter cream (page 206)

blue, green and red colouring

¼ cup (80g) apricot jam, warmed, sieved

DECORATIONS

2 raspberry straps, cut into thin strips

1 teaspoon yellow sprinkles

50 blue M&M's

¼ cup (55g) white sugar

blue colouring

3 sparklers

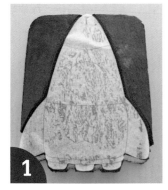

Using paper pattern as a guide, cut out cake.

Cake cut into rocket ship shape.

1 Preheat oven to moderate; grease and line (page 204) deep 26cm x 36cm baking dish. Make cake according to directions on packets, pour into pan; bake in moderate oven about 1 hour. Stand cake in pan 10 minutes; turn onto wire rack to cool. Using serrated knife, level cake top.

2 Turn cake cut-side down. Using paper pattern from pattern sheet, cut out rocket ship; reserve leftover cake. Assemble cake on prepared board, cut-side down, to form rocket ship.

3 Tint a quarter of the butter cream blue. Divide remaining butter cream in half. Tint one half green and the other half red. Using pattern as a guide, spread rocket with green and red butter cream.

4 Use raspberry strips to define and decorate red area. Place 5cm star cutter on cake; cover the area inside cutter with yellow sprinkles, carefully remove cutter.

5 Mark an 8cm circle on cake, press M&M's upright around circle, then fill circle with remaining M&M's.

6 Cut stars from reserved cake, spread sides of stars with warm jam.

7 Place sugar and blue colouring in small plastic bag; rub until sugar is evenly coloured. Lightly sprinkle sides of stars with blue sugar; position around rocket. Spread tops of stars with blue butter cream; sprinkle tops with blue sugar. Position sparklers in cake; light just before serving.

Place star cutter on cake; fill with yellow sprinkles.

Cut stars from reserved cake with star cutter.

Rub colouring into sugar, until sugar is evenly coloured.

express train

CAKE

2 x 340g packets buttercake mix
400g jam roll
22cm x 37cm prepared rectangular
   board (page 206)
2 quantities butter cream (page 206)
green colouring

DECORATIONS

3 raspberry straps
8 Carnival Pops
2 giant green Smarties
1 large yellow gum ball
22 yellow Smarties
8 red Smarties
1 Screw Pop
artificial spider's web

1 Preheat oven to moderate; grease and line
   (page 204) deep 23cm-square cake pan.
   Make cake according to directions on
   packets, pour into pan; bake in moderate
   oven about 1 hour. Stand cake in pan
   10 minutes; turn onto wire rack to cool.
   Using serrated knife, level cake top.

2 Cut square cake in half; cut 2.5cm piece
   from one half of square cake, discard.

3 Cut 3.5cm piece from jam roll, discard.
   Assemble remaining cake pieces on
   prepared board to form train, as shown.

4 Tint butter cream with green colouring;
   spread all over train.

5 Use thin strips of raspberry strap to outline
   train's edges and make window on train.

6 Trim and discard sticks from Carnival
   Pops; position as wheels.

7 Cut six 1.5cm strips from raspberry strap;
   position between wheels as axle. Cut two
   8cm pieces from raspberry strap; position
   at front of train for bumper.

8 Position giant Smarties and gum ball at
   front of train for lights. Decorate train
   with yellow and red Smarties.

9 Place Screw Pop in position for funnel.
   Place a little butter cream on top of
   funnel; press end of a piece of spider's
   web into butter cream for smoke.

TIPS When it comes to eating this cake,
remember that a small segment of stick
is still embedded in each Carnival Pop
(used for wheels).

You can find artificial spider's web at
novelty shops. If you can't find it, use
fairy floss or cottonwool instead. Be sure
to remove spider's web or cottonwool
from cake before cutting and serving.

Cut 2.5cm piece from one half of
square cake and trim 3.5cm piece
from jam roll.

Assemble cakes to form train.

billy the plane

1

Mark and cut cake into shape of plane.

2

Trim cake to make it a more rounded shape.

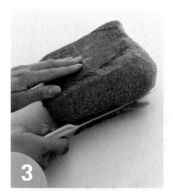

3

Cut cake on an angle from tail end so it appears to be taking off.

4

Write child's name on back of cake, if desired.

CAKE

2 x 340g packets buttercake mix
toothpick
35cm-square prepared board
   (page 206)
1 quantity butter cream (page 206)
red colouring

DECORATIONS

1 black licorice strap
2 large round mints
55g packet M&M's
black glossy decorating gel
1 red oval jube, cut in
   half lengthways
9cm diameter domed plastic
   drink lid

1 Preheat oven to moderate; grease and line (page 204) deep 19cm-square cake pan. Make cake according to directions on packets, pour into pan; bake in moderate oven about 1 hour. Stand cake in pan 5 minutes; turn onto wire rack to cool.

2 Turn cake upside down; using a skewer, mark shape of plane on surface of cake, as shown. Cut cake into plane shape.

3 Cut cake on an angle from the tail end to the front so plane sits back, giving the impression it is taking off.

4 Using small serrated knife, trim cake to make more rounded, trim under wings. Trim a piece of leftover cake to make a tail fin; position on cake with a toothpick.

5 Place cake on prepared board; discard remaining cake pieces.

6 Tint butter cream with red colouring; spread all over plane.

7 Cut two 25cm pieces from licorice strap, roll tightly to make wheels; position under wings. Cut remaining licorice into thin strips for eyebrows and mouth.

8 Position mints for eyes; secure two brown M&M's on mints with a little black decorating gel.

9 Position green M&M for nose and jube halves for propeller. Position yellow M&M on tail.

10 Press plastic lid onto cake. Fill with remaining M&M's.

11 Pipe child's name on back of plane with black decorating gel, if desired.

TIP Be sure to remove toothpick before cutting and serving cake.

1

Trim sides and ends off loaf cakes to form hull.

2

Assemble cake ready to be iced.

lolly goodship

CAKE

3 x 340g packets buttercake mix

34cm x 43cm prepared rectangular
board (page 206)

2 quantities butter cream (page 206)

2 ice-cream cones

green, orange, yellow and
blue colouring

DECORATIONS

6 licorice allsorts

36 five-flavours Life Savers

cottonwool

2 green fruit rings

1 wooden skewer

4 black licorice straps

2 wooden toothpicks

1 Preheat oven to moderate; grease and line
(page 204) two deep 15cm x 25cm loaf pans
and two 8cm x 26cm bar cake pans. Make
cakes according to directions on packets.
Divide two-thirds of the mixture between
loaf pans, divide remaining mixture equally
between bar pans; bake loaf cakes in
moderate oven about 40 minutes and bar
cakes about 25 minutes. Stand cakes in
pans 5 minutes; turn onto wire racks to
cool. Using serrated knife, level cake tops.

2 Trim sides and ends off loaf cakes to form
ship hull, as shown. Position on prepared
board. Round off one end of one bar cake,
cut remaining bar cake in half; position
on top of ship hull to form second deck.
Cut remaining half of bar cake in half
lengthways to make upper deck. Trim
ice-cream cone tops to make funnels;
position on cake.

3 Tint one-third of the butter cream with
green colouring; tint one-third of the
remaining butter cream with orange
colouring, one-third with yellow colouring
and 1 tablespoon with blue colouring.
Reserve remaining butter cream.

4 Spread reserved plain butter cream over
tops of decks and funnels on ship. Spread
sides of hull with green butter cream.
Spread sides of second deck with orange
butter cream. Spread sides of upper deck
with yellow butter cream. Spread blue
butter cream over second deck to make
swimming pool.

5 Cut five allsorts in half (keep one yellow
allsort aside); position allsorts and Life
Savers around sides of ship as portholes.
Press ends of cottonwool onto funnels to
make smoke.

6 Cut green fruit rings open and thread onto
skewer to make mast. Position on ship.

7 Cut licorice strap into thin strips; position
on cake for deck outlines. Position
remaining licorice along top of ship.

8 Cut yellow piece out of remaining allsort,
cut in half diagonally; insert toothpick into
each yellow piece; press into ship for flags.

TIP You will need to buy four 22g packets
of Life Savers for this cake.

Be sure to remove toothpicks, cottonwool
and skewer from cake before cutting
and serving.

choo-choo train

CAKE

2 x 340g packets
   buttercake mix
20cm x 100cm prepared
   rectangular board (page 206)
300g packet jam roll
2 quantities butter cream
   (page 206)
red, blue, yellow, purple and
   green colouring

DECORATIONS

30 ice block sticks
2 black licorice straps
2 tablespoons
   chocolate sprinkles
1 hundreds &
   thousands allsort
8 coloured fruit rings
1 pink ice-cream wafer
1½ cups coloured popcorn
1 yellow chenille stick
   (pipe cleaner)
20 Mint Slices
8 green Smarties
20 pink Smarties
20 orange Smarties
20 red Smarties
20 yellow Smarties

Front view of finished cake.

1   Preheat oven to moderate; grease and
    line (page 204) four 8cm x 26cm bar
    cake pans. Make cakes according to
    directions on packets, divide mixture
    evenly among pans; bake in moderate
    oven about 25 minutes. Stand cakes
    in pans 5 minutes; turn onto wire racks
    to cool. Using serrated knife, level cake
    tops so they are the same height.

2   Place iceblock sticks across prepared
    board. Cut licorice into long thin strips;
    position for track.

3   Cut each bar cake in half vertically; reserve
    five halves to make carriages and back of
    engine. Cut remaining three halves in half
    horizontally; five of these will form bases of
    engine and carriages. Cut one quarter off
    remaining piece to extend engine base;
    discard remaining cake. Cut 4cm piece
    from jam roll; cut 3cm round from piece
    to make smoke stack. Assemble cake
    pieces on prepared board, as shown.

4   Divide butter cream into five portions; tint
    each portion one of the suggested colours:
    red, blue, yellow, purple and green.

5   Spread engine with red butter cream and
    carriages with different coloured butter
    cream. Spread smoke stack with red
    butter cream, roll in chocolate sprinkles;
    place on engine. Place hundreds &
    thousands allsort on engine. Join carriages
    with fruit rings. Outline carriage tops
    and engine with thin strips of licorice.

6   Cut two eyes from licorice strap, position on
    engine. Cut licorice into 5 x 3cm pieces. Cut
    thin strip from ice-cream wafer; position
    at a downwards angle on front of engine.
    Rest licorice pieces on wafer to form grid.

7   Using toothpick or skewer, make small hole
    in 5 pieces of popcorn. Thread popcorn
    onto chenille stick. Position chenille stick
    in top of smoke stack. Fill each carriage
    with remaining popcorn.

8   Position mint slices for wheels. Position
    Smarties on engine and carriages. Secure
    Smarties on wheels with butter cream.

TIP You will need to buy two 200g
packets Mint Slice for this cake.

1

Cut each cake in half vertically.

2

Cut cakes in half horizontally.

3

Cut 3cm round from jam roll.

4

Assemble cake ready to be iced.

candy train

CAKE

2 x 340g packets buttercake mix
¼ cup (25g) cocoa powder
2 cups (320g) icing sugar mixture
10g butter, melted
⅓ cup (80ml) milk
2 cups (180g) desiccated coconut
40cm x 50cm prepared rectangular
    board (page 206)

DECORATIONS

3 green Fruit Sticks, halved
2 green Life Savers
32 yellow Life Savers
2 x 400g packets jelly beans

Top whole lamington with hollowed-out smaller piece to make front of train.

1   Preheat oven to moderate; grease and line (page 204) deep 23cm-square cake pan. Make cake according to directions on packets, pour into pan; bake in moderate oven about 1 hour. Stand cake in pan 10 minutes; turn onto wire rack to cool. Using serrated knife, level cake top.

2   Cut cake into 8 x 6cm squares. Sift cocoa and icing sugar into medium heatproof bowl, stir in butter and milk; stir over medium saucepan of simmering water until icing is of a coating consistency.

3   Using fork, dip squares in icing; drain off excess, toss cakes in coconut. Place lamingtons on wire rack to set.

4   Place one whole lamington at front of prepared board. Cut two-thirds from another lamington; position this lamington piece in front of whole lamington for train's engine. Completely hollow out remaining smaller lamington piece; top whole lamington with hollowed-out lamington, as shown.

5   Using small serrated knife, cut shallow hollows into remaining lamingtons.

6   Connect six lamingtons, hollow-side up, with Fruit Sticks, to make train's carriages.

7   Position green Life Savers on top of engine; position yellow Life Savers on each carriage for wheels. Stand two red jelly beans in green Life Savers on engine; place three black jelly beans at front of engine for grill. Fill each carriage and hollow of engine with remaining jelly beans.

TIP You can use 8 x 6cm-square (3.5cm-deep) ready-made lamingtons, if preferred.

Engine positioned, ready for decoration.

Using a small serrated knife, cut shallow hollows into lamingtons.

teddy bear

CAKE

3 x 340g packets buttercake mix
38cm x 47cm prepared rectangular
    board (page 206)
1 quantity butter cream (page 206)
1 tablespoon cocoa powder
brown colouring

DECORATIONS

22 Smarties
2 dairy milk rounds
1 white marshmallow
1 black licorice strap

1 Preheat oven to moderate; grease and line
   (page 204) two 20cm x 30cm lamington
   pans. Make cakes according to directions
   on packets, divide mixture into prepared
   pans; bake in moderate oven about
   35 minutes. Stand in pans 5 minutes;
   turn onto wire racks to cool. Using
   serrated knife, level cake tops so they
   are the same height.

2 Turn cakes cut-side down. Place cakes
   side by side; using paper pattern from
   pattern sheet, cut out bear.

3 Assemble cake pieces on prepared
   board, cut-side down, as shown.

4 Use a quarter of the butter cream for paws,
   face and tummy.

5 Stir sifted cocoa powder into remaining
   butter cream, tint with brown colouring.
   Spread brown butter cream over cake;
   roughen with fork.

6 Using a little of the butter cream, secure
   two blue Smarties onto the dairy milk
   rounds and position on face for eyes. Cut
   marshmallow in half, position on ears.
   Position a black Smartie for nose. Place
   Smarties on bear for bow tie, as shown.

7 Cut licorice strap into thin strips, position
   on face for mouth and around bow tie.

Place pattern on cake ready to cut.

Assemble cut cake on prepared
board, ready to ice.

spiky echidna
ice-cream cake

CAKE

3.5 litres choc-chip ice-cream,
  softened
1 cream-filled chocolate sponge
  finger, chilled
21cm x 28cm prepared rectangular
  board (page 206)

DECORATIONS

200ml milk chocolate Ice Magic
2 x 200g packets chocolate
  finger biscuits
100g dark eating chocolate,
  grated finely
2 green Smarties

1 Line 2.25-litre (9-cup) pudding steamer
  with plastic wrap; press ice-cream into
  steamer. Cover with foil, freeze 3 hours
  or overnight.

2 Turn steamer upside down on baking-
  paper-lined tray. Remove steamer and
  plastic wrap from ice-cream.

3 Working quickly, trim 2cm from sponge
  finger; position at base of cake for nose.
  Using Ice Magic, coat nose and face in
  chocolate, as shown; stand until chocolate
  is almost set. Using sharp knife, trim away
  any excess chocolate. (Return to freezer
  if necessary.)

4 Working quickly, push finger biscuits into
  ice-cream body; sprinkle grated chocolate
  between biscuits.

5 Using a little Ice Magic, secure Smarties to
  echidna for eyes.

6 Freeze echidna until ready to serve. Using
  egg slide, transfer echidna from baking
  paper to prepared board.

TIP Once the ice-cream softens and
melts slightly, it takes up less space – that
is why 3.5 litres of ice-cream can fit into a
2.25-litre pudding steamer.

Place steamer, upside down, on
baking-paper-lined tray; remove
steamer and plastic wrap.

Using Ice Magic, coat the nose
and face.

Stand cake until chocolate is almost
set, then use a sharp knife to trim
away excess chocolate.

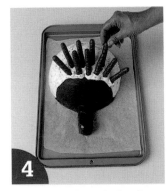

Working quickly, push chocolate
biscuits into the ice-cream cake.

cedric snake

CAKE

2 x 340g packets buttercake mix
30cm x 65cm prepared rectangular
  board (page 206)
1½ quantities butter cream
  (page 206)
purple colouring

DECORATIONS

2 x 350g packets jubes
2 green M&M's
black glossy decorating gel

1 Preheat oven to moderate; grease and line (page 204) two 20cm ring pans. Make cakes according to directions on packets, divide mixture between pans; bake in moderate oven about 35 minutes. Stand cakes in pans 5 minutes; turn onto wire racks to cool.

2 Cut both cakes in half. Assemble pieces on prepared board, as shown.

3 Trim ends to form head and tail.

4 Tint butter cream with purple colouring; spread all over cake.

5 Using a sharp knife, cut jubes in half horizontally. Decorate snake with jubes.

6 Trim one half of a red jube for forked tongue; position on cake.

7 Press green M&M's on cake for eyes. Using black decorating gel, pipe pupils onto M&M's.

TIP Use any soft jubes or jellies you like for the decorations. We preferred ones with very strong colours for a more striking effect.

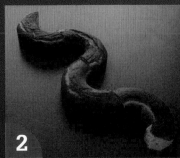

1 Cut both cakes in half; assemble cake halves on board.

2 Use sharp knife to shape spike's head and tail.

dannie dinosaur

CAKE

2 x 340g packets buttercake mix
52cm x 53cm prepared rectangular
    board (page 206)
2 quantities butter cream (page 206)
green colouring

DECORATIONS

37 spearmint leaves
11 Tic Tacs
1 green Life Saver
1 black licorice strap

1   Preheat oven to moderate; grease
    and line (page 204) two 20cm x 30cm
    lamington pans. Make cakes according
    to directions on packets, divide mixture
    evenly between pans; bake in moderate
    oven about 30 minutes. Stand cakes in
    pans 5 minutes; turn onto wire racks to
    cool. Using serrated knife, level cake tops
    so they are the same height.

2   Turn cakes cut-side down. Using paper
    pattern from pattern sheet, cut dinosaur's
    body, tail and legs from cake, as shown.

3   Assemble cake pieces on prepared board,
    cut-side down, as shown.

4   Tint butter cream with green colouring;
    spread all over cake. Create scales using
    a palette knife.

5   Using a sharp knife, cut spearmint leaves
    in half horizontally; position on cake
    for spine.

6   Position trimmed Tic Tacs for teeth and
    Life Saver for eye. Cut licorice strap into
    thin strips, position for eye and mouth.
    Cut claws from remaining licorice strap.
    Position claws on feet.

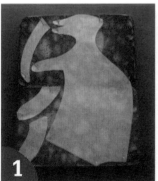

Position paper pattern on cake.

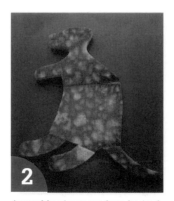

Assemble pieces ready to be iced.

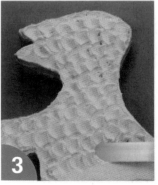

Use a palette knife to make scales.

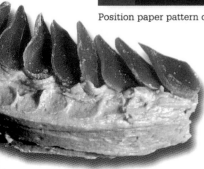

stella stegosaur

CAKE

3 x 340g packets buttercake mix
35cm x 45cm prepared rectangular
    board (page 206)
1 quantity butter cream (page 206)
green colouring

DECORATIONS

8 square After Dinner Mints
3 x 125g boxes chocolate mint sticks
3 x 200g packets spearmint leaves
12 Tic Tacs
1 raspberry strap

1 Preheat oven to moderate; grease and line
(page 204) deep 26cm x 36cm baking
dish. Make cake according to directions on
packets, pour into pan; bake in moderate
oven about 1 hour. Stand cake in pan
10 minutes; turn onto wire rack to cool.
Using serrated knife, level cake top.

2 Turn cake cut-side down. Using paper
pattern from pattern sheet, cut out stella
stegosaur's shape. Position cake on
prepared board cut-side down.

3 Tint butter cream with green colouring;
spread all over cake.

4 Cut After Dinner Mints in half diagonally;
place mints along cake body so they are
raised along the diagonal cut to look like
armoured-plated spikes.

5 Cut mint sticks in graduated lengths;
place in position along back so they
follow the line of the spikes, longer in
the centre, and shorter at the sides.

6 Starting at the tail, cover body and
legs with slightly overlapping spearmint
leaves. Using a sharp knife, cut about
10 mint leaves in half horizontally; place
in position around neck.

7 To decorate face and feet, use Tic Tacs
for claws, a thin piece of raspberry strap
for mouth and a mint stick, thinly sliced,
for eye and nose.

Use paper pattern to cut out cake.

Cut After Dinner Mints in half diagonally.

Using a sharp knife, cut spearmint
leaves in half horizontally.

clara **cro**c**o**dile

CAKE

3 x 340g packets buttercake mix
35cm x 60cm prepared rectangular
board (page 206)
2 quantities butter cream (page 206)
yellow and green colouring

DECORATIONS

30 small lollipops
8 yellow Smarties, cut in half
1 large white marshmallow
1 black licorice strap
1 black jelly bean, cut in half

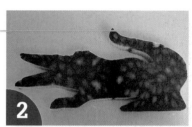

Position pattern on cake ready to be cut.

Cut cake, ready to be iced.

1 Preheat oven to moderate; grease
and line (page 204) two 20cm x 30cm
lamington pans. Make cakes according
to directions on packets. Divide mixture
between pans; bake in moderate oven,
about 35 minutes. Stand cakes in pans
5 minutes; turn onto wire racks to cool.
Using serrated knife, level cake tops so
they are the same height.

2 Turn cakes cut-side down. Cut a 7cm
piece off one end of one cake and assemble
cakes, as shown. Using paper pattern
from pattern sheet, cut out crocodile.
Position cake on prepared board, cut-side
down, as shown; discard remaining cake.

3 Tint ⅓ cup of the butter cream yellow,
tint remaining butter cream green.

4 Spread yellow butter cream over tummy
of crocodile. Spread green butter cream
over remaining cake.

5 Using end of rolling pin, smash lollipops
in small plastic bag to create uneven
sized shards; discard sticks. Shake
broken lollipops through coarse sieve;
discard fine powdered pieces.

6 Sprinkle lollipop shards over crocodile's
back and tail.

7 Position yellow Smarties for teeth. Trim
marshmallow into eye shape; position on
cake. To make eyelashes, cut small piece
of licorice strap into a rectangle, then cut
into thin strips – do not cut all the way
through the strap, as shown. Fan licorice,
position above eye. Position jelly bean on
marshmallow for iris.

8 Cut licorice into six strips for claws.
Position three pieces on each foot.

TIP You will need to buy a 265g packet
of small lollipops for this recipe.

Place lollipops in small plastic bag; use
rolling pin to smash lollipops into shards.

To make eyelashes, cut licorice strap
into small strips.

creepy crawly
spider

Use a toothpick to score baking paper from centre of the cake to end of each segment marking.

Using the markings as a guide, pipe spider's web over top and side of the cake.

Position the steamer cake for spider's body and muffin for spider's head on web.

Spoon remaining purple butter cream into piping bag; pipe stars to cover spider's body.

CAKE

5 x 340g packets buttercake mix
40cm-round prepared board
   (page 206)
5 quantities butter cream (page 206)
green, black and purple colouring

DECORATIONS

9 black bump chenille sticks
1 round licorice allsort
1 orange Skittle
5 red Crazy Bananas

1 Preheat oven to moderate. Grease one hole of 12-hole (⅓-cup/80ml) muffin pan and 1.25-litre (5-cup) pudding steamer; grease and line (page 204) deep 30cm-round cake pan. Make cakes according to directions on packets; pour mixture into muffin hole and pudding steamer until each is three-quarters full. Pour remaining mixture into round cake pan; bake muffin in moderate oven about 20 minutes, steamer cake about 45 minutes and round cake about 1 hour. Stand cakes in pans 10 minutes; turn onto wire racks to cool. Using serrated knife, level steamer and round cake tops.

2 Position round cake on prepared board, cut-side down.

3 Tint three-fifths of the butter cream with green colouring; spread all over round cake.

4 Cut 30cm circle from baking paper; fold baking paper into eight equal segments. Position paper gently on cake; place one toothpick at centre of circle and one toothpick on the outside edge of cake at each segment. Using toothpick, score baking paper from centre of the cake to end of each segment, as shown; remove paper and toothpicks.

5 Tint a quarter of the remaining butter cream with black colouring. Spoon into piping bag (page 209) fitted with 4mm plain tube; using markings as a guide, pipe web over top and side of cake.

6 Position steamer cake, cut-side down, on round cake, as shown, for spider body. Position muffin against body for spider head, as shown.

7 Tint remaining butter cream with purple colouring; spread 2 tablespoons of the purple butter cream over head. Spoon remaining purple butter cream into piping bag fitted with a medium fluted tube; pipe stars to cover body, as shown.

8 Bend eight chenille sticks to form spider legs; position on cake. Cut remaining chenille stick into quarters; position two pieces on cake for pincers.

9 Cut allsort in half; position on cake for eyes. Position Skittle on cake for nose and Crazy Bananas for fangs.

tommy turtle

CAKE

3 x 340g packets buttercake mix
1 cup (150g) white chocolate
    Melts, melted
pink and green colouring
35cm x 45cm prepared rectangular
    board (page 206)
300ml thickened cream
½ cup (160g) strawberry jam
2 quantities butter cream (page 206)

DECORATIONS

1 white marshmallow
blue and black glossy
    decorating gel
1 raspberry strap

1   Preheat oven to moderate; grease and
    line (page 204) deep 26cm x 36cm baking
    dish. Make cake according to directions
    on packets, pour into prepared dish; bake
    in moderate oven about 1 hour. Stand
    cake in dish 10 minutes; turn onto wire
    rack to cool.

2   Tint half of the chocolate light pink and
    the other half dark pink. Using paper
    pattern from pattern sheet as a guide,
    trace the turtle's back onto a piece of
    baking paper. Spoon both chocolates, in
    dollops, onto baking paper within turtle's
    back outline. Using a toothpick or skewer,
    swirl the chocolate dollops together to
    create a marbled effect; allow to set.
    Break set chocolate into pieces.

3   Using paper pattern from pattern sheet, cut
    out cake in turtle shape; reserve leftover
    cake. Position cake on prepared board.

4   Beat cream in small bowl with electric mixer
    until soft peaks form. Cut two-thirds of the
    reserved leftover cake into 2cm pieces; fold
    cake pieces and jam into cream. Spoon
    cream mixture on top of cake to form the
    dome of turtle's back.

5   Tint half the butter cream light green; spread
    all over turtle's back.

6   Tint remaining butter cream dark green;
    spread around feet, flippers, head and
    side of cake.

7   Press chocolate pieces onto cake.

8   To make eyes, cut marshmallow in half
    horizontally; pipe dots with blue and
    black decorating gel to complete eyes;
    position on head. Use a strip of raspberry
    strap to create mouth.

Spoon light pink and dark pink
chocolate onto paper pattern.

Swirl chocolate with a toothpick;
allow to set then break into pieces.

Cut cake ready for decorating.

Spoon cream and cake mixture
onto cake to form turtle shell.

lucy ladybird

CAKE

340g packet buttercake mix
25cm x 30cm prepared rectangular
  board (page 206)
1 quantity butter cream (page 206)
black and red colouring

DECORATIONS

1 black licorice strap
14 chocolate freckles
2 x 15cm (3mm) black chenille
  sticks (pipe cleaners)
2 yellow Smarties

1 Preheat oven to moderate; grease one hole of a 12-hole (⅓-cup/80ml) muffin pan and 1.25-litre (5 cup) pudding steamer. Make cakes according to directions on packet, pour ¼ cup of mixture into prepared muffin hole and remaining mixture into prepared pudding steamer; bake muffin in moderate oven about 20 minutes and large cake about 35 minutes. Stand cakes in pans 5 minutes; turn onto wire rack to cool. Using serrated knife, level large cake top.

2 Using serrated knife, cut segment from muffin. Turn large cake cut-side down; trim dome to make more rounded, as shown. Place cake on prepared board, flat-side down.

3 Tint ¼ cup of butter cream with black colouring and remaining butter cream with red colouring. Spread red butter cream all over body of ladybird.

4 Position muffin against body for head; spread all over with black butter cream. Cut an outside strip of licorice from licorice strap; position along centre of body. Position freckles on body.

5 Curl one end of each chenille stick; position on cake for antennae. Position Smarties on cake for eyes.

Using a serrated knife, trim dome of large cake to make more rounded; cut segment off muffin.

Use a large palette knife to spread the red butter cream all over the ladybird's body.

Position the muffin against the ladybird's body, for head, then spread with black butter cream.

peggy penguin

CAKE

3 x 340g packets buttercake mix
35cm x 45cm prepared rectangular
  board (page 206)
2 quantities butter cream (page 206)
blue, yellow and orange colouring

DECORATIONS

2 slices crystallised orange
1 large round mint
1 red jelly bean
1 black licorice strap
½ x 35g packet pink fairy floss
50cm x 4cm pink wired ribbon

1 Preheat oven to moderate; grease and line (page 204) deep 26cm x 36cm baking dish. Make cake according to directions on packets, pour into prepared pan; bake in moderate oven about 1 hour. Stand cake in pan 10 minutes; turn onto wire rack to cool.

2 Using paper pattern from pattern sheet, cut out penguin. Place cake on prepared board.

3 Tint half the butter cream with the blue colouring. Divide remaining half among three small bowls; tint one with yellow, one with orange and leave the third plain.

4 Spread plain butter cream for tummy, yellow for feet, orange for beak and blue for body.

5 Remove rind from crystallised orange slices; using paper pattern as a guide, cut pieces in shape of beak. Press gently into position.

6 To make eye, place the mint in position, then secure half the red jelly bean to mint with a little butter cream.

7 To make eyelashes, cut licorice strap into a 1.5cm x 3cm rectangle, then cut into thin strips – do not cut all the way through the strap. Fan licorice, position above eye.

8 Using scissors, cut the remaining licorice strap into thin strips. Position strips to outline the stomach, wings, beak and feet.

9 Just before serving, press fairy floss onto stomach. (Fairy floss starts to dissolve after about 1 hour.) Tie ribbon into a bow, position on cake.

Position paper pattern on cake.

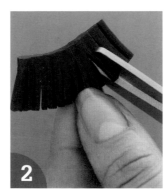

Cut licorice strap into eyelashes.

geraldine *giraffe*

CAKE

3 x 340g packets buttercake mix
35cm x 50cm prepared rectangular
    board (page 206)
1½ quantities butter cream
    (page 206)
orange colouring

DECORATIONS

2 black licorice straps
2 x 75cm long pineapple and orange
    flavoured Troppo Twist fruit
      Roll-Ups reels
toothpick with double-pointed head
6cm piece black licorice twist
1 black jelly bean
1 chocolate bullet
⅔ cup (100g) milk chocolate
    Melts, melted

Position paper pattern on cake
ready to cut out.

1 Preheat oven to moderate; grease deep
26cm x 36cm baking dish, line base
(page 204) with baking paper. Make
cake according to directions on packets;
pour mixture into prepared dish. Bake in
moderate oven about 1 hour. Stand cake
in dish for 10 minutes; turn onto wire
rack to cool. Using serrated knife, level
cake top.

2 Turn cake cut-side down. Using paper
pattern from pattern sheet, cut out body
and head of giraffe. Place cake on prepared
board, cut-side down.

3 Tint butter cream with orange colouring.
Join head and body of giraffe with a little
of the butter cream, spread cake with
remaining butter cream.

4 Cut licorice strap into thin strips; position
licorice around cake.

5 Cut Roll-Ups into three 30cm lengths.
Layer the lengths of Roll-Ups together
to make one thick length; cut thin strips
into the layered Roll-Ups, but not all the
way through, as shown; position on giraffe
for mane. Wrap some of the remaining
Roll-Up around licorice to cover tail; cut
end of Roll-Up to fray end. Secure tail
with toothpick.

6 Cut some of the remaining licorice
strap into thin strips, position on cake
for ear and mouth. Cut licorice twist in
half, position for horns. Cut jelly bean
in half lengthways, position for nose.
Cut chocolate bullet in half, position for
eye. Cut licorice strap into a 1.5cm x 2cm
rectangle, then cut into thin strips – do
not cut all the way through the strap. Fan
licorice, position above eye.

7 Spread melted chocolate evenly on a
piece of baking paper to make a 20cm
square. When chocolate is almost set,
cut into 2.5cm diamond shapes. When
chocolate is completely set, gently lift
diamonds off paper, position on giraffe.

TIP Be sure to remove toothpick from
cake before cutting and serving.

Layer the fruit Roll-Ups together
to make one thick length.

Cut thin strips into the layered
Roll-Ups to make giraffe's mane.

4

Cut licorice strap to make eyelashes, do not cut all the way through.

5

Use ruler to cut chocolate into diamond shapes.

the
penguin prince

CAKE

3 x 340g packets buttercake mix

35cm x 40cm prepared rectangular
   board (page 206)

2 quantities butter cream (page 206)

black, yellow and white colouring

DECORATIONS

2 black Smarties

1 black licorice strap

1 red bow tie

1 Preheat oven to moderate; grease and line (page 204) deep 26cm x 36cm baking dish. Make cake according to directions on packets, pour into prepared dish; bake in moderate oven about 1 hour. Stand cake in dish 10 minutes; turn onto wire rack to cool. Using serrated knife, level cake top.

2 Turn cake cut-side down. Using paper pattern from pattern sheet, cut out penguin. Place penguin on prepared board, cut-side down; discard remaining cake.

3 Using toothpick, and paper pattern as a guide, mark penguin outlines on cake, as shown.

4 Tint half of the butter cream with black colouring, half the remaining butter cream with yellow colouring and remaining butter cream with white colouring.

5 Spread tummy and eyes with white butter cream, feet and beak with yellow butter cream and remaining top and sides of cake with black butter cream.

6 Position Smarties on cake for eyes. Trim licorice strap into thin strip; position on beak. Position bow tie at penguin's neck.

TIP If unable to find white colouring, use plain butter cream, instead.

Turn cake cut-side down. Using the paper pattern, cut penguin from cake, with a serrated knife.

Mark penguin outlines through the paper pattern onto the cake using a toothpick.

Spread the coloured butter creams onto the cake, using the markings as a guide.

leonardo lion

CAKE

3 x 340g packets buttercake mix
35cm x 45cm prepared rectangular
  board (page 206)
2 quantities butter cream (page 206)
orange and yellow colouring

DECORATIONS

2 white marshmallows
2 orange Smarties
black glossy decorating gel
1 red jube, cut in half horizontally
1 black licorice strap

1   Preheat oven to moderate. Grease and line (page 204) 14cm x 21cm loaf pan and two 19cm x 29cm rectangular slice pans. Make cakes separately according to directions on packets; place one quantity of mixture into each of the prepared pans. Bake loaf cake in moderate oven 50 minutes and slice pans 25 minutes. Stand cakes in pans 5 minutes; turn onto wire racks to cool. Using serrated knife, level cake tops.

2   Cut off one-third of cake from one short end of loaf cake. Cut this piece in half horizontally, trim piece into 4cm x 8cm rectangle, then cut point for nose.

3   Place slice pan cakes side by side, cut-side down; trim tops, if necessary, so cakes are the same height.

4   Using paper pattern from pattern sheet, cut out lion's head.

5   Place lion's head on prepared board, cut-side down, top with large oblong from loaf cake, position nose piece on top.

6   Tint ½ cup of the butter cream orange, tint remaining butter cream yellow. Spread yellow butter cream evenly over nose and face and around sides of cake. Spread remaining yellow butter cream thickly for mane. Dot orange butter cream on mane. Using a fork, swirl orange butter cream into yellow butter cream.

7   Position marshmallows and Smarties for eyes. Dot with a little black gel for pupils.

8   Position red jube for tongue.

9   Cut licorice strap into thin strips, position on face for mouth and whiskers. Dot a little black gel near whiskers. Use black decorating gel to draw triangle for nose.

Cut one-third from short end of loaf cake; cut piece in half horizontally, then cut to make nose.

Place slice pan cakes side by side; use paper pattern to cut out lion's head.

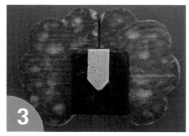

Position large oblong piece from loaf cake and nose piece on top of cake.

Dot orange butter cream on yellow mane; use fork to swirl through butter cream.

timothy tiger

CAKE

2 x 340g packets buttercake mix
40cm-square prepared board
  (page 206)
1½ quantities butter cream
  (page 206)
orange colouring

DECORATIONS

2 white marshmallows
4 orange jubes
1 spearmint leaf
1 smooth black licorice strap

1 Preheat oven to moderate; grease and line
   (page 204) 8cm x 26cm bar cake pan and
   two 19cm x 29cm rectangular slice pans.
   Make cakes according to directions on
   packets, pour 1½ cups of mixture into
   prepared bar cake pan; divide remaining
   mixture evenly between the prepared
   slice pans. Bake bar cake in moderate
   oven about 25 minutes and slice pans
   30 minutes. Stand cakes in pans 5 minutes;
   turn onto wire racks to cool. Using serrated
   knife, level cake tops.

2 Place slice pan cakes side by side, cut-side
   down; trim tops, if necessary, so cakes are
   the same height.

3 Using paper pattern from pattern sheet,
   cut out tiger's head from slice cakes and
   nose from bar cake. Cut nose at an angle,
   as shown. Assemble cake on prepared
   board, cut-side down; position nose.

4 Tint butter cream with orange colouring,
   spread over tiger.

5 Flatten marshmallows with fingers;
   position on cake for eyes. Position
   trimmed jubes for tongue and eyebrows.
   Cut diamond shapes out of spearmint
   leaf, position for pupils.

6 Using pinking shears, cut tiger stripes
   and thin strips for eyes and nose out of
   licorice strap; position on cake.

TIP Pinking shears are available from
sewing or haberdashery shops, however,
you can use straight scissors, if you wish.

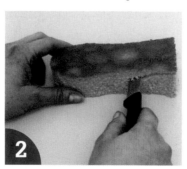

Cut out head and nose of tiger.

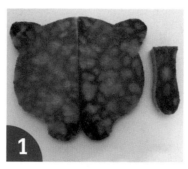

Cut through nose at an angle using a
sharp knife.

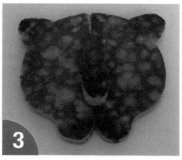

Assemble cake on prepared board, ready
to be iced.

butterfly beauty

CAKE

3 x 340g packets buttercake mix
34cm x 40cm prepared rectangular
   board (page 206)
2 quantities butter cream (page 206)
violet, yellow, pink, green and
   blue colouring

DECORATIONS

34 pink Smarties
26 blue Smarties
35g jar snowflakes
15cm (3mm) mauve chenille
   stick (pipe cleaner)
2 pink lollipops

Position paper pattern on cake, cut out butterfly using a sharp knife.

Use toothpicks to transfer butterfly markings from paper pattern onto cake.

Spread different coloured butter creams on butterfly markings.

1 Preheat oven to moderate; grease and line (page 204) two 19cm x 29cm rectangular slice pans. Make cakes according to directions on packets, divide mixture between prepared pans; bake in moderate oven about 45 minutes. Stand cakes in pans 5 minutes; turn onto wire racks to cool. Using serrated knife, level cake tops so they are the same height.

2 Place cakes together cut-side down. Using paper pattern from pattern sheet, cut out butterfly. Place cake on prepared board, cut-side down.

3 Using toothpicks, transfer markings on paper pattern onto cake.

4 Divide butter cream into three portions, tint one portion with violet colouring and another portion with yellow colouring. Divide remaining butter cream into three smaller portions. Tint one portion pink, one portion green and one portion blue.

5 Spread top and sides of cake with coloured butter creams, using the outlines on the pattern as a guide.

6 Position Smarties around edges of different butter cream colours, decorate with snowflakes. Twist pipe cleaner to resemble antennae; position pipe cleaner and lollipops, as shown.

Wacky wabbit

1

Using paper pattern, cut face and ears from cake.

CAKE

3 x 340g packets buttercake mix

38cm x 52cm prepared rectangular board (page 206)

3 quantities fluffy frosting (page 208)

black colouring

DECORATIONS

icing sugar mixture

200g ready-made soft icing

blue and pink colouring

1 black licorice strap

1 pink marshmallow

6 double-pointed toothpicks

2 milk bottles

2 black Skittles

2

Assemble the cake, cut-side down, to form rabbit.

1 Preheat oven to moderate; grease and line (page 204) deep 26cm x 36cm baking dish. Make cake according to directions on packets, pour into prepared dish; bake in moderate oven about 1 hour. Stand cake in dish 10 minutes; turn onto wire rack to cool. Using serrated knife, level cake top.

2 Turn cake cut-side down. Using paper pattern from pattern sheet, cut out rabbit face and ears from cake. Assemble cake pieces on prepared board, cut-side down, to form rabbit, as shown; discard remaining cake.

3 Spread half the frosting over lower half of rabbit's face; build up frosting around cheeks to make full. Tint remaining frosting with black colouring to make grey; spread over top half of face and ears.

4 On surface dusted with icing sugar, knead soft icing until smooth; roll a quarter of the icing until 3mm thick. Enclose remaining icing in plastic wrap; reserve. Using paper pattern from pattern sheet, cut eyes from white icing; position on cake.

5 On surface dusted with icing sugar, knead blue colouring into half the reserved icing; roll until 3mm thick. Using paper pattern from pattern sheet, cut irises and mouth from blue icing; position on cake.

6 On surface dusted with icing sugar, knead pink colouring into remaining icing; roll until 3mm thick. Using paper pattern from pattern sheet, cut inner ears from pink icing; position on cake.

7 Cut licorice strap into thin strips; outline inner ears, eyes and mouth. Position marshmallow for nose.

8 Cut two 10cm, two 9cm and two 8cm pieces from thinly sliced licorice. Insert one end of each licorice piece with a toothpick; position for whiskers.

9 Trim tops of milk bottles; using a little fluffy frosting, position for teeth. Position Skittles for pupils using a little fluffy frosting.

TIPS Draw inner ear, mouth, eye and iris patterns onto cardboard, then use these templates to cut the shapes from icing.

Be sure to remove toothpicks from cake before cutting and serving.

3

Spread frosting over lower half of face, making thicker around cheeks.

4

Use cardboard templates to cut eyes and mouth from icing.

bruce platypus

CAKE

3 x 340g packets buttercake mix
27cm x 63cm prepared rectangular
    board (page 206)
2 quantities chocolate butter cream
    (page 206)
black colouring

DECORATIONS

1 white marshmallow
1 chocolate mint stick, cut
    into 2 x 5mm rounds
1 black licorice strap

1   Preheat oven to moderate; grease and line
    (page 204) two 15cm x 25cm loaf pans and
    deep 22cm-round cake pan. Make cakes
    according to directions on packets, evenly
    divide two-thirds of the mixture between
    two prepared loaf pans. Spread remaining
    mixture into prepared round cake pan;
    bake round cake pan in moderate oven
    30 minutes and loaf pans 40 minutes. Stand
    cakes in pans 5 minutes; turn onto wire
    racks to cool. Using serrated knife, level
    cake tops so they are the same height.

2   Turn cakes cut-side down. Using paper
    pattern from pattern sheet, carefully cut
    out platypus. Using left-over cake, shape
    into four feet. Assemble cakes on prepared
    board, cut-side down.

3   Tint a quarter of the chocolate butter
    cream with black colouring. Spread black
    butter cream over bill. Spread remaining
    chocolate butter cream over body,
    roughen with a fork.

4   Mark nostrils and mouth in bill.

5   Cut marshmallow in half horizontally; using
    a little butter cream, attach one chocolate
    mint round to each marshmallow half for
    eyes, position on cake.

6   Cut claws from licorice strap; position
    on cake.

Use toothpicks to position paper pattern
on cakes, ready to cut out.

Assemble cake on prepared board ready
for icing.

sammy seal

CAKE

3 x 340g packets buttercake mix
62cm x 85cm prepared rectangular
    board (page 206)
2 quantities butter cream (page 206)
black, orange, blue, green and
    pink colouring

DECORATIONS

1 black licorice strap
1 white marshmallow

1 Preheat oven to moderate; grease and line
   (page 204) three 20cm x 30cm lamington
   pans. Make cakes according to directions
   on packets, divide mixture between
   prepared pans; bake in moderate oven
   about 35 minutes. Stand cakes in pans
   5 minutes; turn onto wire racks to cool.
   Using serrated knife, level cake tops so
   they are the same height.

2 Turn cakes cut-side down. Using paper
   pattern from pattern sheet, cut out seal
   and ball from cake; discard remaining
   cake. Assemble cakes on prepared board,
   cut-side down.

3 Tint two-thirds of the butter cream with
   black colouring to make grey; spread all
   over seal. Using fork, mark seal's skin.
   Tint a quarter of the remaining butter
   cream with orange colouring, a quarter
   with blue colouring, a quarter with green
   colouring and the remaining butter cream
   with pink colouring.

4 Using toothpicks and paper pattern as
   a guide, score ball markings onto cake.
   Spread tinted butter creams over top and
   sides of each ball quadrant.

5 Cut licorice strap into thin strips; position
   on cake for outline of seal, ball, whiskers
   and eyelashes. Cut small piece of the
   licorice for the nose and eye. Trim
   marshmallow to make pupil and tip of
   nose; use a little butter cream to attach
   to licorice. Cut a thin strip of licorice into
   tiny pieces and place around whiskers.

Position paper pattern on cake ready to
be cut out.

Assemble cake on prepared board ready
to be iced.

wobbly wombat

CAKE

3 x 340g packets buttercake mix
½ cup (160g) apricot jam,
   warmed, sieved
30cm-square prepared board
   (page 206)
2 quantities chocolate butter cream
   (page 206)
brown colouring

DECORATIONS

2 milk chocolate Melts
2 black jelly beans
1 square After Dinner Mint
1 Chocolate Monte biscuit
1 black licorice strap

1   Preheat oven to moderate; grease and flour 1.5-litre (6-cup) pudding steamer, 2.5-litre (10-cup) Dolly Varden pan, deep 17cm-round cake pan and two holes of 12-hole (⅓-cup/80ml) muffin pan. Make cakes according to directions on packets, pour ¼ cup of the cake mixture into each prepared muffin hole. Divide remaining cake mixture evenly between prepared pans; bake muffins in moderate oven about 15 minutes, pudding steamer cake about 20 minutes, 17cm cake about 30 minutes and Dolly Varden cake about 40 minutes. Stand cakes in pans 5 minutes; turn onto wire racks to cool. Using serrated knife, level cake and muffin tops.

2   Brush cut-sides of cakes with some of the jam; join cut-sides together to make wombat. Cut muffins in half horizontally. Assemble wombat on prepared board.

3   Tint butter cream with brown colouring to make dark brown; spread all over cake.

4   Using fork, roughen butter cream. Position chocolate Melts for eyes; using a little butter cream, attach jelly beans for pupils. Cut After Dinner Mint in half for ears, position on cake.

5   Position chocolate biscuit on cake for nose. Cut claws from licorice strap; position, as shown.

Assemble cake on prepared board, ready to be iced.

Use a fork to roughen chocolate butter cream on wombat.

wally whale

CAKE

3 x 340g packets buttercake mix
40cm x 45cm prepared rectangular
   board (page 206)
2 quantities butter cream (page 206)
blue colouring

DECORATIONS

½ cup (110g) white sugar
blue colouring
1 black licorice strap
1 blue M&M

1 Preheat oven to moderate; grease and line (page 204) deep 26cm x 36cm baking dish. Make cake according to directions on packets, pour into prepared pan; bake in moderate oven about 1 hour. Stand cake in pan 10 minutes; turn onto wire rack to cool.

2 Using paper pattern from pattern sheet, cut out whale; reserve leftover cake. Cut spout and flipper from reserved cake.

3 Assemble cake on prepared board.

4 Tint half the butter cream with blue colouring. Spread whale's tummy with a little of the plain butter cream. Spread spout with a little of the blue butter cream.

5 Combine remaining blue butter cream and remaining plain butter cream; swirl gently to create a marbled effect. Carefully spread marbled butter cream on cake.

6 Place half the sugar and blue colouring in small plastic bag; rub until sugar is evenly coloured.

7 Sprinkle blue sugar on and around the flipper, tail and tummy. Sprinkle remaining white sugar on spout. Cut a thin strip of licorice strap for mouth and place in position. Cut eye from remaining licorice; position on cake. Secure blue M&M on licorice with a little butter cream.

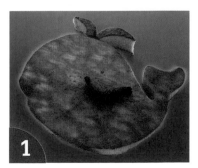

Assemble whale on prepared board, ready to ice.

Swirl blue butter cream and plain butter cream together to create marbled effect.

françois ze frog

CAKE

3 x 340g packets buttercake mix
40cm-square prepared board
   (page 206)
2 quantities butter cream (page 206)
green and red colouring

DECORATIONS

14 brown Smarties
2 red Smarties
18 red frogs
18 green frogs
1 green and yellow bow

1 Preheat oven to moderate; grease and line (page 204) deep 26cm x 36cm baking dish. Make cake according to directions on packets, pour into prepared pan; bake in moderate oven about 1 hour. Stand cake in pan 10 minutes; turn onto wire rack to cool. Using serrated knife, level cake top.

2 Turn cake cut-side down. Using paper pattern from pattern sheet, cut out frog's body and eyes from cake.

3 Assemble cake pieces on prepared board, cut-side down, to form frog; discard remaining cake.

4 Reserve 2 tablespoons of the plain butter cream for eyes. Tint three-quarters of the remaining butter cream with green colouring; tint remaining butter cream with red colouring. Spread green butter cream all over cake.

5 Carefully place paper pattern on cake for eyes, face and front legs; using toothpick, mark outline on cake.

6 Spoon red butter cream into piping bag (page 209) fitted with 4mm plain tube; pipe over marked outlines and around edge of frog. Pipe smile on face.

7 Spread reserved plain butter cream on eyes; position brown Smarties for pupils and toes. Position red Smarties for nose. Position red and green frogs around side of cake; position bow under frog's chin.

Turn cake cut-side down. Position paper pattern, then cut frog's body and eyes from cake.

Assemble the cake pieces on board, cut-side down, to form frog; discard remaining cake.

3 Place patterns on cake for eyes, face and front legs; using a toothpick, mark outline on cake.

4 Place red butter cream into piping bag; pipe over marked outlines and around edge of frog.

tennis court

CAKE

3 x 340g packets buttercake mix
35cm x 45cm rectangular prepared
   board (page 206)
1 quantity butter cream (page 206)
brown colouring

DECORATIONS

icing sugar mixture
500g packet ready-made soft icing
blue colouring
2m x 2mm-wide white ribbon
1 egg white, beaten lightly
20cm netting
12 double-pointed toothpicks
3 black licorice straps
½ cup (75g) white chocolate
   Melts, melted
¼ cup (35g) dark chocolate
   Melts, melted
1 raspberry strap, cut into thin strips
1 fruit Roll-Ups
8 small mints
1 Mint Slice
8 spearmint leaves

To make umpire's chair, insert
licorice strap into toothpicks.

Use melted chocolate to outline
tennis racquets and strings.

Wrap strips of fruit Roll-Ups around
handles of tennis racquets.

1 Preheat oven to moderate. Grease and
   line (page 204) deep 26cm x 36cm baking
   dish. Make cake according to directions
   on packets, pour into dish; bake in moderate
   oven about 1 hour. Stand cake in dish
   10 minutes; turn onto wire rack to cool.
   Using serrated knife, level cake top.

2 Place cake on prepared board, cut-side
   down. Tint butter cream with brown
   colouring; spread all over cake.

3 On a surface dusted with icing sugar,
   knead soft icing until smooth. Knead blue
   colouring into icing. Roll out icing evenly
   into a piece large enough to cut out a
   15cm x 32.5cm rectangle; carefully centre
   rectangle on cake.

4 Cut ribbon into 4 x 32.5cm, 2 x 11.6cm,
   2 x 15cm and 1 x 17.4 cm lengths. Brush
   backs of ribbons lightly with egg white;
   press onto court, as shown. Secure net
   onto cake with toothpicks.

5 Cut four 10cm pieces from licorice strap. Pipe
   Happy Birthday on two of the straps using
   melted white chocolate. Join remaining

pieces to back of signs, along top edges,
with melted dark chocolate. Outline with
raspberry strips. Position on cake.

6 To make umpire's chair, cut two 2cm pieces
   of black licorice strap. Push two toothpicks
   through back of licorice seat, and attach
   the other piece of licorice for chair back,
   as shown. Push another two toothpicks
   for front legs. Position chair on cake.

7 Draw four tennis racquets on baking
   paper; pipe dark melted chocolate for
   racquet frame. Pipe racquet strings with
   white melted chocolate. When set, peel
   off paper and wrap narrow strips of fruit
   Roll-Ups around racquet handles. Position
   on cake with small mints for balls.

8 Place Mint Slice in one corner; attach two
   spearmint leaves with a little dark melted
   chocolate. Skewer remaining spearmint
   leaves with toothpicks; position along
   side of cake, as pictured.

TIP Be sure to remove toothpicks from
cake before cutting and serving.

Fun & Games

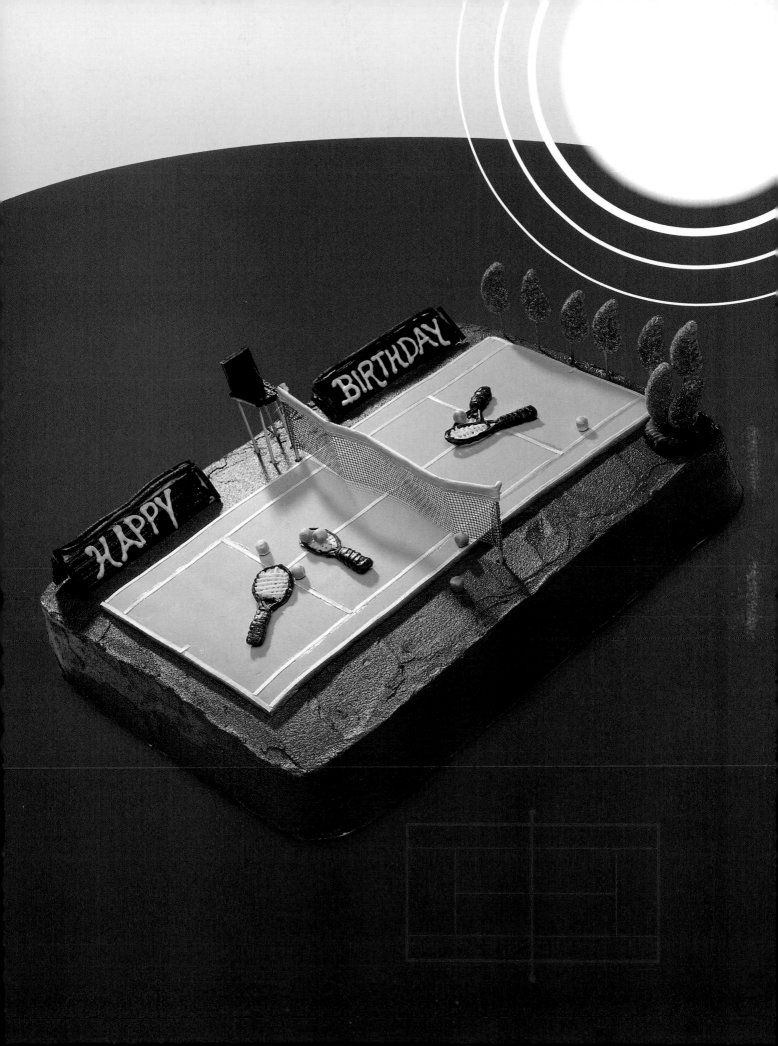

trampoline

CAKE

2 x 340g packets buttercake mix
33cm-round prepared board
    (page 206)
1 quantity butter cream (page 206)
green colouring

DECORATIONS

3 x 250g packets Fruit Sticks
icing sugar mixture
500g ready-made soft icing
yellow colouring
18cm cardboard circle
4 x 60g packets Chunky
    Raspberry Twisters
assorted dolls

1 Using the markings as a guide, cut a shallow hollow into the cake with a small serrated knife.

2 Tint the butter cream with green colouring; using a palette knife, spread all over the cake.

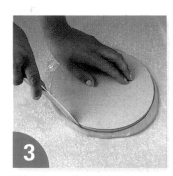

3 Using the cardboard circle as a guide, cut a circle from the icing with a sharp-pointed knife.

4 Cut Raspberry Twisters in half lengthways then into 2.5cm pieces; trim the edges on an angle.

1   Preheat oven to moderate; grease and line (page 204) deep 22cm-round cake pan. Make cake according to directions on packets, pour into pan; bake in moderate oven about 1 hour. Stand cake in pan 5 minutes; turn onto wire rack to cool. Using serrated knife, level cake top.

2   Position cake on prepared board, cut-side down. Using ruler and toothpicks, mark a 17cm circle in centre of cake. Using markings as a guide, cut shallow hollow into cake with small serrated knife.

3   Tint butter cream with green colouring; spread all over cake.

4   Trim Fruit Sticks to the same height as cake; position around side of cake.

5   On surface dusted with icing sugar, knead soft icing until smooth. Knead yellow colouring into icing; roll until 5mm thick. Using cardboard circle as a guide, cut circle from icing with sharp-pointed knife; position on cake to cover hollow. Enclose remaining icing in plastic wrap.

6   Cut Raspberry Twisters in half lengthways; cut halves into 2.5cm pieces. Trim edges of pieces on an angle; position on cake for springs.

7   On surface dusted with icing sugar, roll reserved icing into long, 5mm-thick rope; position around outside top edge of cake. Position dolls as desired.

play poOl

CAKE

2 x 340g packets buttercake mix
35cm-round prepared board
 (page 206)
½ cup (160g) apricot jam,
 warmed, sieved

DECORATIONS

85g packet blue jelly crystals
icing sugar mixture
1kg ready-made soft icing
purple, green, yellow, pink and
 blue colouring
2 dolls

Using markings as a guide, cut a shallow hollow from the cake with a serrated knife.

Roll the icing into a rope long enough to reach around the circumference of the cake.

Position half of the blue icing around the top edge of the play pool.

Shape the reserved icings into pool toys, but don't position in the pool until serving the cake.

1 Preheat oven to moderate; grease and line (page 204) deep 22cm-round cake pan. Make cake according to directions on packets, pour into pan; bake in moderate oven about 1 hour. Stand cake in pan 5 minutes; turn onto wire rack to cool. Using serrated knife, level cake top.

2 Make jelly according to directions on packet; refrigerate until almost set.

3 Position cake on prepared board, cut-side down. Using ruler and toothpicks, mark a 19cm circle in centre of cake. Using markings as a guide, cut 2cm-deep hollow from cake with small serrated knife. Brush top edge and side of cake with jam.

4 On surface dusted with icing sugar, knead soft icing until smooth. Knead purple colouring into 200g of the icing; roll three-quarters of the purple icing into a rope long enough to reach around the bottom circumference of cake. Enclose remaining purple icing in plastic wrap. Position rope around cake. Repeat with 200g batches of icing and green, yellow and pink colouring, stacking the coloured ropes up the outside of the cake.

5 Knead blue colouring into remaining white icing; roll half of the icing into a rope long enough to reach around the top edge of the cake. Flatten rope slightly with rolling pin; position on cake for top of pool. Roll remaining blue icing into a rope long enough to reach around the circumference of the cake; position on cake above pink rope, as shown.

6 When jelly is almost set, stir gently to break up; spoon into hollowed section of cake. Position dolls in pool.

7 On surface dusted with icing sugar, shape reserved rolled icings into pool toys; position in and around pool just before serving.

TIP It's important not to position the pool toys in the pool until just before serving the cake, because they will dissolve soon after they touch the jelly.

go 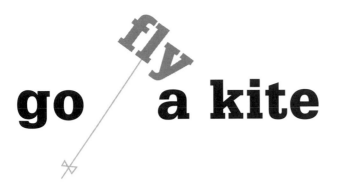 a kite

CAKE

3 x 340g packets buttercake mix
34cm x 43cm prepared rectangular
  board (page 206)
2½ quantities butter cream
  (page 206)
yellow, red, green and orange
  colouring

DECORATIONS

1 black licorice strap
50cm red ribbon
50cm purple ribbon
50cm orange ribbon
50cm green ribbon
1m rope
icing sugar mixture
250g ready-made soft icing

1 Preheat oven to moderate; grease and line (page 204) deep 26cm x 36cm baking dish. Make cake according to directions on packets, pour into dish; bake in moderate oven about 1 hour. Stand cake in dish 10 minutes; turn onto wire rack to cool. Using serrated knife, level cake top.

2 Turn cake cut-side down. Using paper pattern from pattern sheet, cut kite from cake. Position cake on prepared board, cut-side down; discard remaining cake.

3 Place two lines of toothpicks in cake, connecting opposing corners of kite, as shown. Divide butter cream among four small bowls. Tint one bowl of butter cream with yellow colouring, one with red colouring, one with green colouring and one with orange colouring.

4 Using toothpicks as a guide, spread tinted butter creams over top and side of kite quadrants; remove and discard toothpicks.

5 Cut licorice strap into thin strips; position around each coloured quadrant and edge of kite.

6 Using coloured ribbons, tie bows onto rope; position on board.

7 On surface dusted with icing sugar, knead ready-made icing until smooth; roll icing until 3mm thick. Using 4cm and 5cm flower cutters, cut clouds from icing; position on board around kite.

1 Place the cake cut-side down then, using the paper pattern, cut kite from cake.

2 Using toothpicks as a guide, spread coloured butter creams over the kite quadrants.

3 Roll icing until 3mm thick then, using flower cutters, cut clouds from the icing.

up, up & away

1 Using a small serrated knife, trim the tops of the cakes to make them more rounded.

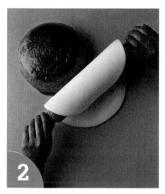

2 When icing is large enough to cover the cake, carefully lift icing over cake using a rolling pin.

CAKE

3 x 340g packets buttercake mix
½ cup (160g) apricot jam,
    `warmed, sieved
52cm-round prepared board
    (page 206)

DECORATIONS

icing sugar mixture
2.5kg ready-made soft icing
pink, green and blue colouring
1m x 2cm-wide pink ribbon
1m x 2cm-wide blue ribbon
1m x 2cm-wide green ribbon

1 Preheat oven to moderate; grease and line (page 204) three deep 20cm-round cake pans. Make cakes according to directions on packets, divide mixture among pans; bake in moderate oven about 40 minutes. Stand cakes in pans 5 minutes; turn onto wire racks to cool.

2 Using small serrated knife, trim cake tops to make more rounded, as shown. Brush jam all over cakes.

3 On surface dusted with icing sugar, knead soft icing until smooth; knead pink colouring into a third of the icing. Reserve a walnut-sized amount for balloon end; enclose in plastic wrap.

4 Using rolling pin, roll remaining pink icing into circle large enough to cover one cake. Using rolling pin, lift icing over one cake; using sharp-pointed knife, neatly trim excess icing. Position cake on prepared board.

5 Using hands dusted with icing sugar, gently mould icing into balloon shape.

6 On surface dusted with icing sugar, make balloon end from reserved pink icing. Using toothpick or skewer, make creases in balloon end, as shown. Gently push balloon end into balloon; attach to cake with a tiny dab of water. Carefully wrap ribbon around balloon end.

7 Repeat with remaining cakes, icing, colouring and ribbons.

3 Dust your hands with icing sugar then gently mould the icing into a balloon shape.

4 On a surface dusted with icing sugar, mould the balloon end from the reserved icing.

5 Using a toothpick or skewer, make small creases in the underside of the balloon end.

hOwdy sheriff

CAKE

3 x 340g packets buttercake mix
35cm-square prepared board
  (page 206)
2 quantities butter cream (page 206)
yellow and red colouring

DECORATIONS

6 chocolate freckles
42 silver cachous

1 Preheat oven to moderate; grease and line (page 204) deep 30cm-square cake pan. Make cake according to directions on packets, pour into pan; bake in moderate oven about 1 hour 15 minutes. Stand cake in pan 10 minutes; turn onto wire rack to cool. Using serrated knife, level cake top.

2 Turn cake cut-side down. Using paper pattern from pattern sheet, cut badge from cake. Place on prepared board, cut-side down; discard remaining cake.

3 Tint two-thirds of the butter cream with yellow colouring; spread all over cake.

4 Tint remaining butter cream with red colouring; spoon into piping bag (page 209) fitted with 4mm plain tube; pipe half the red butter cream around edges of badge.

5 Position freckles on badge. Using tweezers, decorate cake with cachous.

6 Pipe name onto cake with remaining red butter cream.

1 Turn cake cut-side down. Using the paper pattern, cut sheriff's badge from cake.

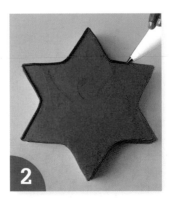

2 Using a piping bag, pipe the red butter cream around edges of sheriff's badge.

3 Pipe the birthday child's name onto sheriff's badge with the remaining red butter cream.

merry-go-round

CAKE

3 x 340g packets
 buttercake mix
¼ cup (80g) apricot
 jam, warmed, sieved
33cm-round prepared
 board (page 206)

DECORATIONS

cardboard cylinder
16 x 20cm (6mm-wide) assorted
 coloured ribbons
8 x 25cm-long thick bamboo
 skewers, trimmed to 20cm
8 x 18cm (6mm-wide) assorted
 coloured ribbons
8 small unpainted craftwood horses

icing sugar mixture
1.5kg ready-made soft icing
pink colouring
22cm circle thick cardboard
1 egg white
1½ cups (240g) pure icing sugar
2 x 250g packets Fruit Sticks
2 x 15g packets Fizzers
glue gun
2 x 15g packets coloured cachous

This cake is not difficult – it is, however, time consuming.

1 Preheat oven to moderate; grease one hole of six-hole texas (¾-cup/180ml) muffin pan, and grease and line (page 204) two deep 22cm-round cake pans. Make cakes according to directions on packets, pour one-third of the mixture into one round pan, ½-cup mixture into prepared muffin hole and remaining mixture into other round pan. Bake muffin in moderate oven about 25 minutes, shallow cake about 30 minutes and deep cake about 50 minutes. Stand cakes in pans 5 minutes; turn onto wire racks to cool. Using serrated knife, level top of deep cake.

2 Trim cardboard cylinder to 20cm. Using sticky tape, secure two 20cm ribbons to one end of a skewer; wrap ribbon around skewer, as shown. Secure other end with tape. Repeat with remaining 20cm ribbons and skewers. Tie 18cm ribbons around necks of horses.

3 Brush cakes all over with jam. On surface dusted with icing sugar mixture, knead soft icing until smooth. Knead pink colouring into icing; roll half the icing until large enough to cover deep cake. Enclose remaining icing in plastic wrap; reserve.

4 Using rolling pin, place icing over cake; trim around base of cake. Position cake on prepared board. Roll three-quarters of the reserved icing until large enough to cover shallow cake. Using rolling pin, place icing over cake; trim around base of cake. Position

shallow cake on cardboard circle. Roll remaining icing until large enough to cover muffin. Using rolling pin, place icing over muffin; trim around base of muffin.

5 Cut 22cm circle from baking paper; fold baking paper into eight equal wedges. Position paper on deep cake; using toothpick, score paper through to icing on wedge-shaped tracings, alternately at 1.5cm and 5cm points from outside edge of cake, as shown. Discard paper.

6 Push cardboard cylinder through the centre of the deep cake to the board. Insert one ribbon-wrapped skewer into each toothpick marking, making sure the skewers and cardboard cylinder are of the same height.

7 Stir egg white and sifted pure icing sugar together in small bowl until smooth. Brush cardboard cylinder all over with egg-white mixture; position 14 Fruit Sticks upright against cylinder. Decorate top of cylinder with Fizzers.

8 Centre muffin on top of shallow cake; carefully centre shallow cake on top of skewers and cylinder. Using glue gun, secure one horse to each skewer.

9 Using egg-white mixture, decorate carousel with remaining Fruit Sticks and cachous. Use Fruit Stick trimmings to make stars; position on cake using egg-white mixture.

TIPS We painted the horses with non-toxic paint.

The cardboard cylinder must be strong – we used the inside of a baking-paper roll.

1 Wrap two 20cm ribbons around each skewer, securing with tape.

2 Score baking paper and icing with a toothpick to make eight markings.

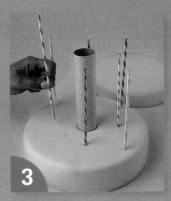

3 Position one ribbon-wrapped skewer into each toothpick marking.

4 Carefully centre the shallow cake on skewers and cardboard cylinder.

treasure island

CAKE

3 x 340g packets buttercake mix
36cm x 46cm prepared rectangular
    board (page 206)
2 quantities butter cream (page 206)
green, yellow and blue colouring

DECORATIONS

2 x 35g tube mini M&M's
1 tablespoon brown sugar
1 waffle cone
red and black glossy decorating gel
28 chocolate-covered fruit and nuts
small plastic animals
small plastic trees

1   Preheat oven to moderate; grease and
    line (page 204) deep 26cm x 36cm baking
    dish. Make cake according to directions
    on packets, pour into baking dish; bake
    in moderate oven about 1 hour. Stand
    cake in pan 5 minutes; turn onto wire
    rack to cool.

2   Place cake on prepared board, top-side up.
    Using melon baller or small teaspoon,
    scoop about five deep holes into cake,
    reserve scoops of cake. Fill holes with half
    the M&M's; top with reserved cake.

3   Tint half the butter cream with blue colouring;
    tint one-third of the remaining butter cream
    with yellow colouring. Tint two-thirds of the
    remaining butter cream green. Reserve
    remaining plain butter cream.

4   Cover top of island with green butter
    cream. Spread yellow onto a few edges
    of island to resemble the beach; sprinkle
    yellow butter cream with brown sugar to
    resemble sand. Swirl blue butter cream
    with plain butter cream; spread over
    remaining cake to resemble water.

5   Break tip off waffle cone, push cone into
    cake for volcano; fill volcano with remaining
    M&M's through peak. Using red decorating
    gel, pipe around top of cone to make lava.

6   Position chocolate-covered fruit and nuts
    to form paths. Position animals and trees
    on island. Using black decorating gel,
    mark a black cross for the treasure.

TIP You will need to buy a 300g packet
of chocolate-covered fruit and nuts for
this cake.

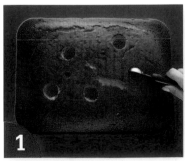

Using a melon baller, or small teaspoon,
scoop out holes in cake.

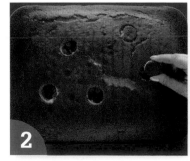

Fill the holes with mini M&M's. Push
reserved cake into holes to hide treasure.

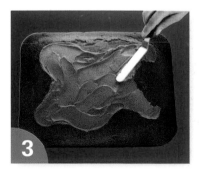

Cover top of cake with green
butter cream.

party piñata

Using the markings as a guide, cut a deep hollow into the cake with a small serrated knife.

Spread the chocolate butter cream over the cake, then fill the hollow with coins and rainbow choc-chips.

Swirl the chocolate around the inside of the steamer until it is evenly coated.

When set, use a hot cloth to briefly rub bowl to remove the shell.

Allow the birthday child to break open the chocolate shell with a toy hammer.

CAKE

340g packet buttercake mix

30cm-round prepared board (page 206)

1 quantity chocolate butter cream (page 206)

DECORATIONS

23 large chocolate coins

19 medium chocolate coins

13 small chocolate coins

150g rainbow choc-chips

½ teaspoon vegetable oil

450g milk chocolate Melts, melted

50g milk eating chocolate, melted

35g tube mini M&M's

250g packet M&M's

toy hammer

1 Preheat oven to moderate; grease and line (page 204) deep 15cm-round cake pan. Make cake according to directions on packet, pour into pan until three-quarters full; bake in moderate oven about 45 minutes. Stand cake in pan 5 minutes; turn onto wire rack to cool.

2 Position cake on prepared board. Using ruler and toothpicks, mark 11cm circle in centre of cake. Using markings as a guide, cut deep hollow into cake with a small serrated knife.

3 Spread chocolate butter cream all over cake; fill hollow with coins and half of the rainbow choc-chips.

4 To make chocolate shell: grease 2.25-litre (9-cup) pudding steamer with oil; place bowl in freezer 10 minutes. Place melted chocolate Melts in steamer; swirl chocolate to coat inside of steamer evenly. Continue swirling until chocolate begins to set and stops flowing around the steamer; try to keep the chocolate a uniform thickness, particularly at the top edge. Stand until chocolate is almost set. Freeze until chocolate sets completely.

5 Carefully place pudding steamer with set chocolate shell over cake; using hot cloth, briefly rub outside of bowl. Chocolate shell will slip from bowl to completely enclose cake.

6 Using melted milk chocolate, secure remaining rainbow choc-chips, mini M&M's and M&M's to chocolate shell.

7 Allow birthday child to break chocolate shell open with toy hammer.

TIP Make patty cakes from any leftover cake mixture.

sam the tool man

CAKE

2 x 340g packets buttercake mix
45cm-square prepared board
   (page 206)
1 quantity butter cream (page 206)
blue colouring

DECORATIONS

icing sugar mixture
200g ready-made soft icing
yellow colouring
candy cake decorations
assorted toy tools

Cut the hat's peak from the plain icing, then mould it around the front edge of the cake.

1 Preheat oven to moderate; grease 1.75-litre (7-cup) pudding steamer. Make cake according to directions on packets, pour into steamer until three-quarters full; bake in moderate oven about 50 minutes. Stand cake in steamer 5 minutes; turn onto wire rack to cool. Using serrated knife, level cake top.

2 Place cake on prepared board, cut-side down.

3 On surface dusted with icing sugar, knead soft icing until smooth; roll half of the icing until 3mm thick. Cut hat peak from icing; mould around cake.

4 Tint butter cream with blue colouring; spread all over cake and peak.

5 Knead yellow colouring into remaining icing; roll three-quarters of the icing into thick rope. Position around edge of hat.

6 Roll remaining icing until 3mm thick; cut out name plaque. Position name and desired candy cake decorations on plaque using a little water; position plaque on hat.

7 Place assorted toy tools around cake on board.

TIP Make patty cakes from any leftover cake mixture.

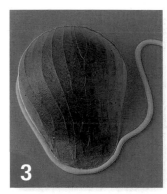

Tint the butter cream blue, then spread it over the cake and hat peak with a palette knife.

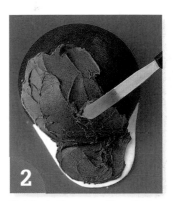

Roll three-quarters of the yellow icing into a thick rope. Position rope around edge of hat.

chessboard

CAKE

340g packet buttercake mix
33cm-square prepared
    board (page 206)
1 quantity butter cream (page 206)

DECORATIONS

icing sugar mixture
500g ready-made soft icing
2 black licorice straps
chess pieces

1 Preheat oven to moderate. Grease and
line (page 204) 23cm-square slab pan.
Make cake according to directions on
packet, pour into pan; bake in moderate
oven about 35 minutes. Stand cake in
pan 10 minutes; turn onto wire rack to
cool. Using serrated knife, level cake top
and trim sides to make square.

2 Place cake on prepared board, cut-side
down. Spread butter cream evenly over
top and sides of cake.

3 On surface dusted with icing sugar,
knead soft icing until smooth. Using
rolling pin, roll icing until slightly larger
than top of cake. Trim icing to fit top of
cake exactly, carefully lift icing onto cake.

4 Cut licorice into 32 squares. Press
licorice squares gently into icing to
create chessboard. Cut four strips of
licorice to cover each side of the cake.
Position licorice around sides of cake.

5 Arrange chess pieces on cake.

1

Trim sides of cake to make square.

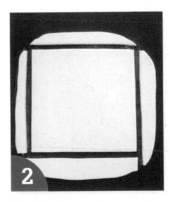

2

Trim icing to same size as cake top.

one teddy and his bed

Leave one bar cake whole. Cut the other bar cake into three pieces, as shown.

Assemble cake pieces on the board to form the number one; discard remaining cake.

CAKE

340g packet buttercake mix

23cm x 51cm prepared rectangular board (page 206)

1 quantity butter cream (page 206)

blue colouring

1 Preheat oven to moderate; grease and line (page 204) two 8cm x 26cm bar cake pans. Make cake according to directions on packet, divide mixture between pans; bake in moderate oven about 25 minutes. Stand cakes in pans 5 minutes; turn onto wire racks to cool. Using serrated knife, level cake tops so cakes are the same height.

2 Turn cakes cut-side down. Cut one cake into three pieces, as shown. Assemble cake pieces on prepared board, cut-side down, to form the number one; discard remaining cake.

3 Tint butter cream with blue colouring; spread all over cake.

4 On surface dusted with icing sugar, knead soft icing until smooth. Roll half of the icing until 3mm thick, cut 11cm square for sheet; cover sheet and enclose white trimmings in plastic wrap.

DECORATIONS

icing sugar mixture

250g ready-made soft icing

yellow, green and pink colouring

22 coloured cachous

small teddy bear

5 Knead yellow colouring into remaining icing; roll until 3mm thick. Using pastry wheel and ruler, cut 10cm square for quilt; enclose yellow trimmings in plastic wrap. Using ruler, mark 2.5cm intervals on all four quilt edges. Using pastry wheel, ruler and markings as guides, gently roll wheel across icing to make quilt pattern.

6 Using tiny cutters or sharp-pointed knife, cut moon and star shapes from quilt, as shown; cover quilt with plastic wrap. Position some of the shapes at top of cake with 10 of the cachous. Shape yellow trimmings into pillow, place on cake. Position sheet on cake, top with quilt; turn down edge.

7 Divide reserved white trimmings in half. Knead green colouring into one half of the white trimmings and pink into the other half; roll each until 3mm thick. Using tiny cutters or sharp-pointed knife, cut out heart shapes; position with remaining cachous on cake. Position bear near pillow.

TIPS One year olds may be too young to eat the cachous, but they'll certainly love the cake.

Tiny heart-, star-, moon- and other-shaped cutters are sometimes sold as aspic cutters.

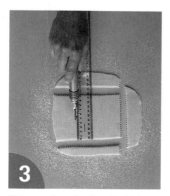

Using pastry wheel and ruler as a guide, cut a 10cm square from yellow icing for quilt.

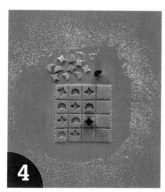

Use tiny cutters or a small sharp-pointed knife to cut shapes from the quilt.

taller at two

CAKE

2 x 340g packets buttercake mix
35cm x 45cm prepared rectangular
    board (page 206)
2 quantities butter cream (page 206)
orange colouring
¼ cup (25g) cocoa powder

DECORATIONS

¼ cup (55g) white sugar
yellow colouring
1 black licorice strap
1 white marshmallow
1 green allsort
blue glossy decorating gel
2 double-pointed toothpicks
2 spearmint leaves
2 TeeVee Snacks

1 Preheat oven to moderate; grease and line (page 204) 20cm x 30cm lamington pan and 8cm x 26cm bar cake pan. Make cakes according to directions on packets; divide mixture between pans so that both mixtures are the same depth. Bake lamington pan in moderate oven about 35 minutes and bar pan about 25 minutes. Stand cakes in pans 5 minutes; turn onto wire racks to cool. Using serrated knife, level cake tops so cakes are the same height.

2 Turn cakes cut-side down. Using paper pattern from pattern sheet, cut cake, as shown. Assemble cake pieces on prepared board, cut-side down, to form the number two; discard remaining cake.

3 Tint three-quarters of the butter cream with orange colouring; spread over cake.

4 Place sugar and yellow colouring in small plastic bag; rub until sugar is evenly coloured. Sprinkle over cake.

5 Combine remaining butter cream and sifted cocoa in small bowl. Spoon into piping bag (page 209); pipe spots onto cake.

6 Cut licorice strap into thin strips; position strips to outline cake and mouth.

7 Cut marshmallow in half, discard one half; place green allsort on top of remaining half. Pipe dot with blue decorating gel on allsort to complete eye; position on head.

8 Insert toothpicks into base of spearmint leaves; press into head for ears.

9 Position TeeVee Snacks next to mint leaves, to resemble horns.

TIP Be sure to remove toothpicks from cake before cutting and serving.

Cut out cake using paper pattern.

Insert toothpicks into base of leaves.

fishes for three 3

CAKE

2 x 340g packets buttercake mix
25cm x 40cm prepared rectangular
    board (page 206)
2 quantities butter cream (page 206)
blue colouring

DECORATIONS

2 teaspoons white sugar
blue colouring
4 apricot fruit Roll-Ups
36 blue Smarties
1 black licorice strap
4 Mentos
red glossy decorating gel
5 ice-cream wafers
1 tablespoon orange sprinkles

1

Cut cakes into segments, as shown.

Shape and assemble cut cake in
the shape of the number three.

1 Preheat oven to moderate; grease and
   line (page 204) two 20cm ring pans. Make
   cakes according to directions on packets,
   divide mixture between pans; bake in
   moderate oven about 35 minutes. Stand
   cakes in pans 5 minutes; turn onto wire
   racks to cool. Using serrated knife, level
   cake tops so cakes are the same height.

2 Turn cakes cut-side down; cut and shape
   segments from cakes, as shown.

3 Assemble cake pieces on prepared board,
   cut-side down, to form the number three;
   discard remaining cake.

4 Tint one-third of the butter cream pale
   blue; tint remaining butter cream darker
   blue. Spread pale blue butter cream over
   both ends of the cake, as shown. Reserve
   1 tablespoon of the dark butter cream,
   spread remainder over remaining cake.

5 Place sugar and blue colouring in
   small plastic bag; rub until sugar is
   evenly coloured. Sprinkle over pale
   blue butter cream.

6 Cut two Roll-Ups into four fin-shaped
   pieces. Form into two fins by joining
   pieces together with a little water, trim
   if necessary. Place fins at the start of the
   dark blue icing on each end. Cut two
   5cm x 9cm triangles from Roll-Ups. Join
   triangles together with a little water, place
   on cake at centre of the figure to form
   a tail. Cut four 1cm x 6cm strips from
   remaining Roll-Ups, shape one end into a
   curve; join two pieces with a little water.
   Place on cake to resemble mouths.

7 Position Smarties on dark blue butter
   cream to resemble scales. Cut licorice
   strap into thin strips; position on cake
   to outline fins, tails and mouths. Place
   Mentos on heads for eyes, pipe eyeballs
   with red decorating gel.

8 Cut wafers in half on the diagonal;
   position two pieces on heads of fish and
   eight pieces as spines. Spread reserved
   butter cream over wafers; sprinkle with
   orange sprinkles.

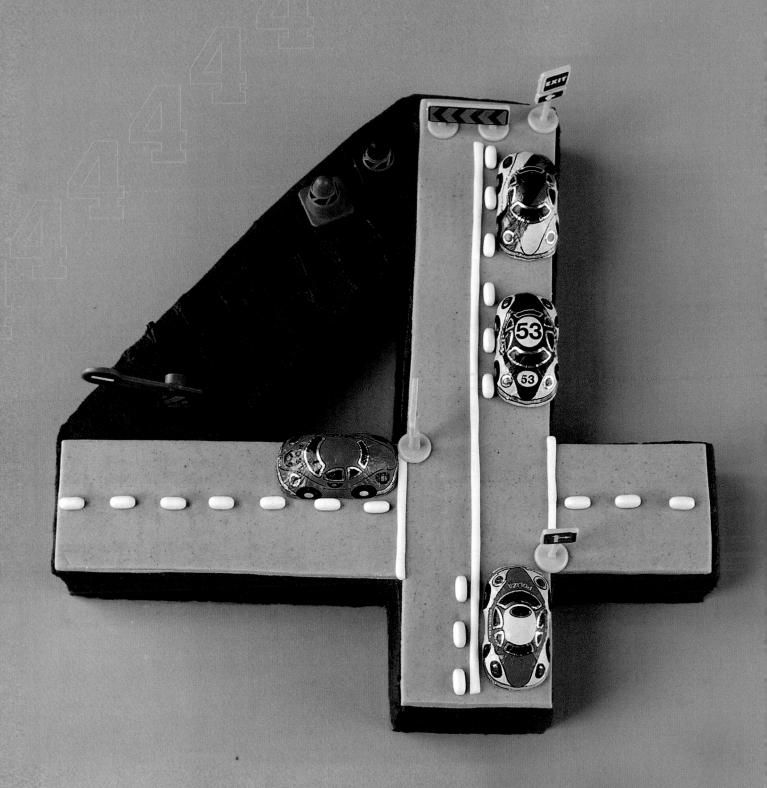

four racing cars

CAKE

2 x 340g packets buttercake mix
40cm-square prepared board
   (page 206)
1½ quantities butter cream
   (page 206)
red colouring

DECORATIONS

icing sugar mixture
250g ready-made soft icing
black colouring
19 Tic Tacs
1 black licorice strap
4 chocolate cars
assorted mini road signs

1 Preheat oven to moderate; grease and line (page 204) 20cm x 30cm lamington pan. Make cake according to directions on packets, pour into prepared pan; bake in moderate oven about 40 minutes. Stand cake in pan 5 minutes; turn onto wire rack to cool. Using serrated knife, level cake top.

2 Turn cake cut-side down. Cut cake into three even strips, as shown.

3 Leave centre strip whole; cut remaining strips into three segments, as shown.

4 Assemble cake pieces on prepared board, cut-side down, to form the number four; discard remaining cake.

5 Tint butter cream with red colouring; spread all over cake.

6 On surface dusted with icing sugar, knead soft icing until smooth; reserve a walnut-sized amount of icing for road markings, enclose in plastic wrap.

7 Knead black colouring into remaining icing to make grey colour; roll until 2mm thick. Using sharp knife, cut 6.5cm x 28cm rectangle, 6.5cm x 15cm rectangle and 6.5cm x 8cm rectangle; position on cake for roads.

8 Roll reserved white icing into thin cord, cut into two 6.5cm pieces and one 27cm piece; secure to cake, with tiny dabs of water, for road markings.

9 Secure Tic Tacs to roads with tiny dabs of water to mark lanes. Cut licorice strap into fourteen 1cm pieces and one 13cm piece; position on cake to form rail tracks. Position cars and road signs on cake, as desired; secure with a little butter cream.

1 Turn cake cut-side down. Using a serrated knife, cut the cake into three even strips.

2 Leave the centre strip whole; cut the two remaining strips into segments, as shown.

3 Assemble the cake pieces on the board to form the number four; discard remaining cake pieces.

five meringue grubs

MERINGUE GRUBS

1 egg white
¾ cup (165g) caster sugar
¼ teaspoon cream of tartar
2 tablespoons boiling water
coloured sprinkles
10 coloured cachous

CAKE

340g packet buttercake mix
30cm x 45cm prepared
   rectangular board (page 206)
1½ quantities butter cream
   (page 206)
pink colouring

DECORATIONS

36 mini pink Musk Sticks
36 love hearts
1 green Fruit Stick
11 spearmint leaves

Using a piping bag, pipe five grubs onto oven tray.

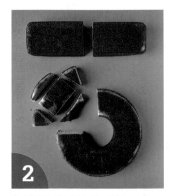

Cut bar cake in half widthways; cut ring cake into small segments, as shown.

Assemble cake pieces on board to form the number five; discard remaining cake pieces.

1 To make meringue grubs: preheat oven to very slow. Combine egg white, sugar, cream of tartar and the boiling water in small bowl. Bring small saucepan of water to a boil; reduce heat to a simmer. Place bowl over saucepan, taking care that water level does not touch bottom of bowl. Beat egg-white mixture with electric mixer about 7 minutes or until sugar is dissolved and stiff peaks form. Remove bowl from heat; spoon egg-white mixture immediately into large piping bag (page 209) fitted with 1cm plain tube. Pipe five grubs onto oven tray lined with baking paper. Top grubs with coloured sprinkles; position cachous on grubs for eyes. Bake in very slow oven about 30 minutes or until grubs are dry to touch; cool.

2 Preheat oven to moderate; grease and line (page 204) 8cm x 26cm bar cake pan and 20cm ring pan. Make cake according to directions on packet; divide mixture between pans so both mixtures are the same depth. Bake in moderate oven about 25 minutes. Stand cakes in pans 5 minutes; turn onto wire racks to cool. Using serrated knife, level cake tops so cakes are the same height.

3 Turn cakes cut-side down. Cut bar cake in half widthways; cut ring cake, as shown.

4 Assemble cake pieces on prepared board, cut-side down, to form the number five; discard remaining cake.

5 Tint butter cream with pink colouring; spread all over cake.

6 Position meringue grubs on cake; decorate sides of cake with Musk Sticks and love hearts. Thinly slice Fruit Stick lengthways; position on cake for stems. Using a sharp knife, cut spearmint leaves in half horizontally; cut a few "nibbles" out of a leaf or two. Position leaves on cake.

TIP Grubs can be made up to a week ahead; store in an airtight container.

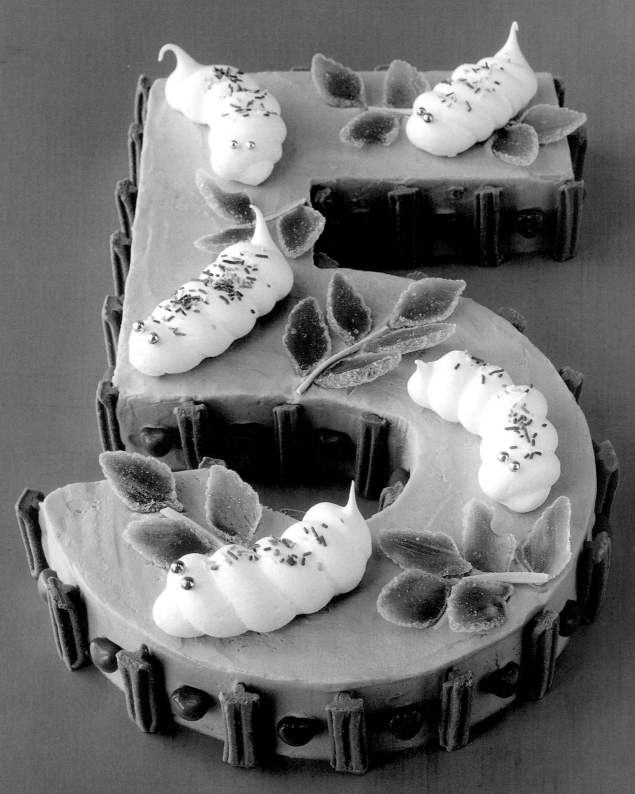

six little devils

CAKE

340g packet buttercake mix

30cm x 44cm prepared rectangular board (page 206)

1½ quantities butter cream (page 206)

black and red colouring

DECORATIONS

2 bananas

8cm fruit Roll-Ups

1 black licorice strap

2 green M&M's

1 milk bottle, halved lengthways

1 Preheat oven to moderate; grease and line (page 204) 8cm x 26cm bar cake pan and 20cm ring pan. Make cake according to directions on packet; divide mixture between pans so both mixtures are the same depth. Bake in moderate oven about 25 minutes. Stand cakes in pans 5 minutes; turn onto wire racks to cool. Using serrated knife, level cake tops so they are the same height.

2 Turn cakes cut-side down. Using paper pattern from pattern sheet, cut tail from bar cake.

3 Assemble cake pieces on prepared board, cut-side down, to form the number six; discard remaining cake.

4 Tint one-quarter of the butter cream with black colouring; spread over widow's peak and end of tail. Tint remaining butter cream with red colouring; spread over remaining cake.

5 Trim banana ends diagonally; position on cake for horns. Cut eyes from fruit Roll-Ups; position on cake. Cut 8cm piece from licorice strap; outline eyes. Position M&M's on cake for pupils.

6 Cut eyebrows, mouth and goatee from remaining licorice; position on cake. Trim milk bottle halves for fangs; position on cake.

1 Leave ring cake whole; lay paper pattern on bar cake for devil's tail.

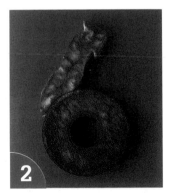

2 Assemble cake pieces on board to form the number six.

seven
choc-crackle spiders

Leave one bar cake whole, cut the other into two pieces, as shown.

Assemble cake pieces on prepared board, cut-side down, to form the number seven.

Twist four chenille sticks together at centre; bend the ends to make spider legs.

CHOC-CRACKLE SPIDERS

1 cup (35g) Rice Bubbles
1 cup (70g) shredded coconut
1 tablespoon cocoa powder
1 tablespoon icing sugar mixture
100g dark eating chocolate, melted
30g butter, melted

CAKE

340g packet buttercake mix
31cm x 47cm prepared rectangular
    board (page 206)
1 quantity butter cream (page 206)
orange and black colouring

DECORATIONS

28 x 15cm (3mm) black chenille
    sticks (pipe cleaners)
14 Skittles

1 To make choc-crackle spiders: combine Rice Bubbles, coconut, sifted cocoa and icing sugar in medium bowl. Using fork, mix in chocolate and butter. Spoon level tablespoons of mixture into two 12-hole mini (1 tablespoon/20ml) muffin tins. Refrigerate about 1 hour or until spider bodies have set.

2 Preheat oven to moderate; grease and line (page 204) two 8cm x 26cm bar cake pans. Make cake according to directions on packet, divide cake mixture between pans; bake in moderate oven about 25 minutes. Stand cakes in pans 5 minutes; turn onto wire racks to cool. Using serrated knife, level cake tops so they are the same height.

3 Turn cakes cut-side down. Cut one cake into two pieces, as shown. Assemble cake pieces on prepared board, cut-side down, to form the number seven.

4 Tint three-quarters of the butter cream with orange colouring; spread all over cake. Tint remaining butter cream with black colouring; spoon into piping bag (page 209) fitted with 2mm plain nozzle, pipe spider webs onto cake and board.

5 Twist four chenille sticks together at centre; bend ends to make spider legs. Position legs on cake; top with one spider body.

6 Using leftover butter cream, attach Skittles onto spider for eyes; pipe a little black icing on Skittles for pupils. Repeat with remaining chenille sticks, spider bodies, black butter cream and Skittles.

TIPS Chocolate and butter can be melted together over hot water or in a microwave oven on HIGH (100%) for about 1 minute.

This recipe makes 24 choc-crackle spiders; serve the extras as an accompaniment or, if you have extra chenille sticks and Skittles, make more spiders to decorate the cake board, or give one spider to each guest.

8 eight octopus

CAKE

2 x 340g packets buttercake mix
30cm x 48cm prepared rectangular
  board (page 206)
2 quantities butter cream (page 206)
purple and aqua colouring

DECORATIONS

¼ cup (35g) white chocolate
  Melts, melted
8 Killer Pythons
85g packet blackcurrant jelly
  crystals
¼ cup (20g) desiccated coconut
purple colouring
1 black licorice strap
3 white chocolate Melts, extra
2 green Smarties

RIGHT EYE

LEFT EYE

1   Preheat oven to moderate; grease and
    line (page 204) two 20cm ring pans. Make
    cakes according to directions on packets,
    divide mixture between pans; bake in
    moderate oven about 35 minutes. Stand
    cakes in pans 5 minutes; turn onto wire
    racks to cool. Using serrated knife, level
    cake tops so they are the same height.

2   Meanwhile, using pattern on this page,
    trace two 3cm x 4cm eyes on a sheet
    of baking paper; turn paper over so
    outlines are underneath. Place melted
    chocolate in piping bag (page 209). Pipe
    eyes onto baking paper, as shown;
    refrigerate until set.

3   Turn cakes cut-side down. Trim a shallow
    arc from one cake, as shown. Assemble
    cake pieces on prepared board, cut-side
    down, to form the number eight; discard
    remaining cake.

4   Reserve about 1 teaspoon of butter cream.
    Tint half the remaining butter cream with
    purple colouring; spread over top and side
    of head. Tint remaining butter cream with
    aqua colouring; spread over top and side
    of remaining cake.

5   Position Pythons around octopus chin,
    pressing gently into butter cream.

6   Combine jelly crystals, coconut and purple
    colouring in small plastic bag; rub until
    mixture is evenly coloured. Sprinkle
    mixture over face and top of tentacles.

7   Cut licorice into thin strips; outline mouth
    around hole in centre of head. Position
    extra Melts for teeth. Position eyes on
    head; position Smarties for pupils, using
    a little of the reserved butter cream.

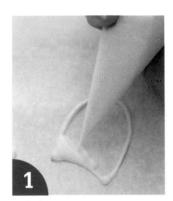

Pipe eyes onto a sheet of baking
paper with melted white chocolate.

Leave one cake whole; trim shallow
arc from the edge of other cake.

Assemble cake on prepared board
to form the number eight.

Combine jelly crystals, coconut and
purple colouring in small bag.

nine ladybirds

CAKE

340g packet buttercake mix

30cm x 49cm prepared rectangular
board (page 206)

1½ quantities butter cream (page 206)

green colouring

DECORATIONS

9 chocolate ladybirds

9 spearmint leaves

Leave ring cake whole; cut bar cake
into three segments, as shown.

Assemble cake pieces to form the
number nine.

1 Preheat oven to moderate; grease and
line (page 204) 8cm x 26cm bar cake pan
and 20cm ring pan. Make cake according
to directions on packet; divide cake
mixture between pans so both mixtures
are the same depth. Bake in moderate
oven about 25 minutes. Stand cakes in
pans 5 minutes; turn onto wire racks to
cool. Using serrated knife, level cake tops
so they are the same height.

2 Turn cakes cut-side down. Cut bar cake
into three pieces, as shown. Assemble
cake pieces on prepared board, cut-side
down, to form the number nine; discard
remaining cake.

3 Tint butter cream with green colouring;
spread three-quarters of the butter cream
over cake.

4 Tint remaining butter cream with more
colouring to make a deeper green. Spoon
into piping bag (page 209) fitted with
4mm plain nozzle; pipe vine and tendrils
onto cake. Position chocolate ladybirds
and spearmint leaves on cake.

ten & soda pizza

Cut loaf cake in shape of soda glass.

Red icing positioned on soda glass cake.

Place white icing around round cake.

Cut unevenly into icing on top of round cake.

CAKE

2 x 340g packets buttercake mix
35cm x 50cm prepared rectangular
　board (page 206)

DECORATIONS

500g ready-made soft icing
icing sugar mixture
red colouring
½ cup (160g) strawberry jam

4 (2.5cm x 4cm) pieces
　turkish delight
1 curly straw
3 cake stars
white glossy decorating gel
1 teaspoon cocoa powder
1 tablespoon water
yellow colouring
¼ cup (15g) shredded coconut
7 black jelly beans
5 Fruit Fantasy Strawberries
1 sour apple karate belt

1 Preheat oven to moderate; grease and line (page 204) deep 22cm-round cake pan and 15cm x 25cm loaf pan. Make cakes according to directions on packets; divide mixture between pans so both are the same depth. Bake cakes in moderate oven about 35 minutes. Stand cakes in pans 5 minutes; turn onto wire racks to cool. Using serrated knife, level cake tops so they are the same height.

2 Turn cakes cut-side down. Using paper pattern from pattern sheet, cut out soda glass from loaf cake. Assemble cakes on prepared board, cut-side down.

3 Divide soft icing into a 290g portion, a 200g portion and a 10g portion.

4 On surface dusted with icing sugar, knead 290g portion of soft icing until smooth. Knead red colouring into icing; roll until large enough to cover loaf cake. Cut one side of icing straight. Carefully lift icing and place over loaf cake, placing cut edge 3cm below top of cake. Using hands dusted with icing sugar, gently mould icing over loaf cake; trim edges.

5 Brush ¼ cup of the jam over uniced part of soda glass cake.

6 Roll 10g portion of soft icing into 20cm-long cord. Position at top of soda glass cake to create a rim on the glass, trim ends.

7 Rinse icing sugar off turkish delight; pat dry with absorbent paper. Cut each turkish delight into small cubes. Press turkish delight onto strawberry jam. Push curly straw into soda glass.

8 Decorate glass with cake stars. Using white decorating gel, pipe a swirl onto soda glass.

9 Roll 200g portion of soft icing into 5cm x 80cm rectangle. Carefully lift and place icing around edge of round cake. Using hands dusted with icing sugar, gently mould icing over edge of cake, trim edge. Using a small knife, cut unevenly into icing on top of round cake. Blend cocoa powder with water in small bowl. Brush over icing to resemble pizza crust.

10 Spread centre of round cake with remaining strawberry jam.

11 Place a few drops of yellow colouring in small bowl; add 2 teaspoons of water. Add coconut; toss gently to colour coconut unevenly. Scatter coconut over strawberry jam on round cake to represent cheese.

12 Position jelly beans and strawberries over coconut to create olive and pepperoni topping. Cut sour apple karate belt into curvy strips; position randomly over coconut to resemble green capsicum.

We used packet cake mixes throughout this book to ensure consistency of size and texture. However, if you would prefer to make your own cake, we have included four fabulously easy and delicious recipes in these information pages to use as your starting point.

NB The patterns supplied for cakes on the pattern sheet are of actual size.

Making the cake

For best results:

● Use an electric mixer when beating the cake mixture.
● Follow the directions on the packet.
● Have all ingredients at room temperature.
● A large mixing bowl should have the capacity to hold 4 packet mixes. It's best to mix single packets in a small bowl, and 2 or 3 packets in a medium bowl.

Baking cakes together

You can bake cakes together, either on the same oven shelf or on different shelves. The important thing is that the cake pans do not touch each other, the sides of the oven or the door. If baking cakes on the same shelf, exchange the positions of the pans about halfway through the baking time.

If you are baking cakes on different shelves, make certain there is enough room for the cake on the lower shelf to rise without touching the bottom of the shelf above. Change the cakes from the lower to the upper shelf positions about halfway through baking time for even browning.

When small cakes are baked with larger cakes (which have longer baking times), place the small cakes toward the front of the oven then, when the small cakes are baked, move the large cakes into that position to complete their baking time.

When two or more cakes are being baked in the oven at the same time, the baking time may be slightly longer than specified in the recipes.

A perfectly baked cake should feel firm to the touch and be slightly shrunken from the side(s) of the pan. There should not be any need to test with a skewer. However, if in doubt, test by inserting a metal skewer into the centre of the cake; if any mixture clings to the skewer, the cake needs a little more baking time. Never test a sponge cake with a skewer; instead, gently press the surface of the cake with fingertips – it should feel firm.

cutting paper

lining base and side of tin

Cake pans

Each recipe specifies the required pan size(s) and exact quantities required to make your cakes look the same as ours. However, cake sizes and shapes can be changed to suit yourself and your chosen decorations. Use rigid, straight-sided, deep cake pans. The ones we used are made from good-quality tin or aluminium.

Greasing and lining the cake pan

All cake pans were greased lightly but evenly with a pastry brush dipped in a little melted butter. An alternative method is to spray pans with cooking-oil spray. We lined the bases of the pans with baking paper. To fit baking paper, place your pan, right-side up, on a piece of baking paper, then trace around the pan's base with a pencil. Cut the paper shape just slightly inside the marked area, to allow for the thickness of the pan. We also lined the side(s) of the cake pans so the paper extended above the pan.

Cake recipes

Each of these recipes makes a cake equal in quantity to one 340g packet of White Wings Golden Buttercake Cake Mix. Therefore, if the particular recipe you've decided to make calls for 2 packets of cake mix, double the quantities called for and adjust the baking time. These four cake recipes will bake in approximately the same time as the packet mixes.

Basic buttercake

125g butter, softened
½ teaspoon vanilla extract
¾ cup (165g) caster sugar
2 eggs
1½ cups (225g) self-raising flour
½ cup (125ml) milk

Preheat oven to moderate. Grease (and line) pan(s).

Beat butter, extract and sugar in small bowl with electric mixer until light and fluffy. Beat in eggs, one at a time, until combined. Stir in flour and milk, in two batches. Spread mixture into prepared pan(s). Bake in moderate oven until cake is cooked. Stand cake in pan(s) 5 to 10 minutes; turn onto wire rack to cool.

To marble a butter cake, place portions of cake mixture in different bowls then tint each with desired colour. Dollop spoonfuls of mixture into prepared pan(s), alternating colours, then gently swirl together with a skewer or spoon, to create a marbled effect.

Rich chocolate cake

1⅓ cups (200g) self-raising flour
½ cup (50g) cocoa powder
125g butter, softened
½ teaspoon vanilla extract
1¼ cups (275g) caster sugar
2 eggs
⅔ cup (160ml) water

Preheat oven to moderate. Grease (and line) pan(s).

Sift flour and cocoa into medium bowl, add remaining ingredients; beat on low speed with electric mixer until ingredients are combined. Increase speed to medium; beat about 3 minutes or until mixture is smooth and changed to a lighter colour. Spread into prepared pan(s). Bake in moderate oven until cake is cooked. Stand cake in pan(s) 5 to 10 minutes; turn onto wire rack to cool.

Best-ever sponge

The only liquid called for in this recipe comes from the eggs; for best results, they should be at room temperature.

3 eggs
½ cup (110g) caster sugar
¼ cup (35g) wheaten cornflour
¼ cup (35g) plain flour
¼ cup (35g) self-raising flour

Preheat oven to moderate. Grease (and line) pan(s).

Beat eggs in small bowl with electric mixer until thick and creamy (this will take about 8 minutes). Add sugar, 1 tablespoon at a time, beating after each addition, until sugar dissolves; transfer mixture to large bowl. Sift dry ingredients together three times then sift evenly over egg mixture; fold in gently. Spread into prepared pan(s). Bake in moderate oven until cake is cooked. Turn immediately onto wire rack to cool.

Wheat-free sponge

This is a gluten-free cake, perfect for people who suffer from coeliac disease and do not tolerate wheat flour. Cornflour, also called cornstarch in some countries, is made from corn kernels and contains no gluten. Use care when purchasing cornflour because there is a wheaten cornflour available which, as the name suggests, contains wheat.

3 eggs
½ cup (110g) caster sugar
¾ cup (110g) cornflour (100% corn)

Preheat oven to moderate. Grease (and line) pan(s).

Beat eggs in small bowl with electric mixer until thick and creamy (this will take about 8 minutes). Add sugar, 1 tablespoon at a time, beating after each addition until sugar dissolves. Sift cornflour three times then sift evenly over egg mixture; fold in gently. Spread into prepared pan(s). Bake in moderate oven until cake is cooked. Turn immediately onto wire rack to cool.

Preparing the cake(s)

Trim cooked cake(s) so it sits flat or joins neatly to another cake.

trimming cake with serrated knife

Most cakes in this book use the smooth base as the top of the finished cake; in this case, it's a good idea to cool the cake upside down. Some cakes are decorated top-side up.

Crumbs can present problems when they become mixed with the icing. To prevent this from happening, bake cake the day before you decorate it. After the cake cools, keep it in an airtight container in the refrigerator overnight. Decorate cake while it is still cold. If you think you will take longer than 30 minutes to decorate your cake, freeze it, uncovered, for about 30 minutes, before decorating.

Cake boards

Most of the cakes in this book call for a cake board which becomes part of the decoration. In any case, the board makes the cake easy to handle as well as more attractive.

Place cake(s), as directed, on a board that has been covered with greaseproof decorative paper, contact, or any type of patterned foil-like gift wrapping. We've given an approximate cake-board size in almost all of the recipes, allowing some space around the cake. Using masonite or a similarly strong board, cut your selected paper 5cm to 10cm larger than the shape of the board. A variety of sizes of boards can be bought, already covered in paper, from cake-decorating suppliers and some craft shops.

Using paper patterns

If you choose to make a cake that is based on a pattern, you will find the template on the pattern sheet in this book. Using a pencil, trace the pattern onto baking or greaseproof paper. Carefully cut around this paper tracing. Assemble cake pieces as directed in the recipe method, then place the paper pattern on top of cake.

Using toothpicks, secure pattern onto cake. Using a small serrated knife, cut around the pattern to form the shape of the cake. Remove toothpicks and pattern, then proceed with recipe.

If you are cutting shapes from ready-made soft icing using a paper pattern, use the above method, but do not use toothpicks to secure the pattern to icing. Use a small sharp-pointed knife to cut around the pattern.

If you are cutting shapes from fabric using a paper pattern, use the original method to create the pattern, then use pins to attach the pattern to fabric and scissors to cut around pattern.

Choosing the covering

We used either butter cream, ready-made soft icing or fluffy frosting, depending on the effect we desired. Ready-made soft icing is easy to use and gives a smooth surface to the cake. Butter cream is a little harder to spread than fluffy frosting, but you can work with butter cream longer than with fluffy frosting, which tends to set. Fluffy frosting is good for fluffy or snowy effects, but it is fairly difficult to make smooth.

The yellow colour of the butter cream will affect the colour you choose. For example, if you add rose pink, the cream tends to become salmon pink; if you add red, it becomes apricot and so on. If you use ready-made soft icing or fluffy frosting, you have a white base to colour from.

Use a spatula or palette knife for spreading and swirling butter cream or fluffy frosting.

Butter cream

This is a basic butter cream (also known as vienna cream) recipe; the flavour can be varied by adding finely grated rind of any citrus fruit or any essence to your taste.

125g butter, softened
1½ cups (240g) icing sugar mixture
2 tablespoons milk

Beat butter in small bowl with electric mixer until as white as possible. Gradually beat in half of the icing sugar, milk, then remaining icing sugar. Flavour and colour as required. *Chocolate variation*: Sift ⅓ cup (35g) cocoa powder in with the first batch of icing sugar.

Ready-made soft icing

Ready-made soft icing is available from cake-decorating suppliers and some health-food shops, delicatessens and supermarkets. There are several brands available, and they can be sold as Soft Icing, Prepared Icing or Ready-to-Roll

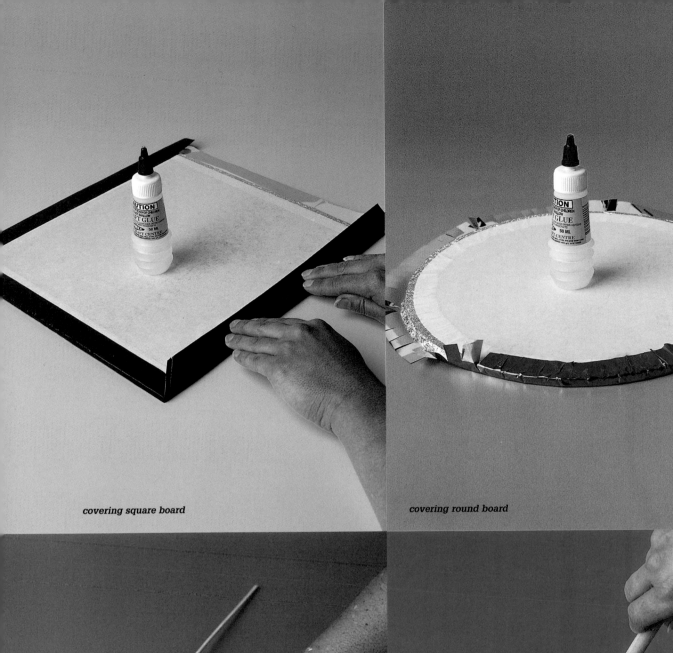

covering square board

covering round board

kneading colouring into ready-made soft icing

colouring butter cream

Icing. All are easy to handle; knead the icing gently on a surface dusted with icing sugar mixture until it is smooth.

Brush warmed strained apricot jam lightly and evenly all over cake. Roll icing until it is about 7mm thick. Lift icing onto cake with rolling pin. Smooth the icing with hands dusted with icing sugar, easing it around the side(s) and base of cake. Push icing in around the base of cake then cut away any excess with a sharp knife.

Fluffy frosting

1 cup (220g) caster sugar
⅓ cup (80ml) water
2 egg whites

Combine sugar and the water in small saucepan; stir with a wooden spoon over high heat, without boiling, until sugar dissolves. Boil, uncovered, without stirring, about 3 to 5 minutes or until syrup is slightly thick. If a candy thermometer is available, the syrup will be ready when it reaches 114°C (240°F).

When the syrup is thick, or has reached the correct temperature, remove the pan from the heat, allow the bubbles to subside then test the syrup by dropping 1 teaspoon into a cup of cold water. The syrup should form a ball of soft sticky toffee when rolled gently between your fingertips. The syrup should not change colour; if it does, it has been cooked for too long and you will have to discard it and start again.

While the syrup is boiling, beat the egg whites in a small bowl with an electric mixer until stiff; keep beating (or whites will deflate) until syrup reaches the correct temperature.

When syrup is ready, allow bubbles to subside then pour a very thin stream onto the egg whites with mixer operating on medium speed. If syrup is added too quickly to the egg whites, frosting will not thicken.

Continue beating and adding syrup until all syrup is used. Continue to beat until frosting stands in stiff peaks (frosting should be barely warm by this stage).

Tint frosting, if desired, by beating food colouring through while mixing, or by stirring through with spatula at the end. Frosting also can be flavoured with a little of any essence of your choice.

For best results, frosting should be applied to a cake on the day it is to be served, while the frosting is still soft and has a marshmallow consistency. While you can frost the cake the day before, the frosting will become crisp and lose its glossy appearance, much like a meringue.

Make sure to frost the cake around the base near the board; this forms a seal and helps keep the cake fresh.

Piping gel

Piping gel is sold in small tubes at supermarkets. If you prefer, make your own using the recipe below. Store the mixture in an airtight container in the refrigerator for up to a month; if it becomes too thick, stir in a tiny amount of water, a little at a time, until gel reaches a piping consistency.

⅓ cup (75g) caster sugar
1 tablespoon cornflour
¼ cup (60ml) lemon juice
¼ cup (60ml) water

Combine sugar and cornflour in small saucepan; gradually blend in juice then the water. Stir over high heat until mixture boils and thickens. Colour piping gel as desired.

pouring syrup onto egg whites

Equipment

Piping bags can be bought from cake-decorating or chefs' suppliers; these are usually made from a waterproof fabric, and can have screws attached to hold icing tubes.

Alternatively, you can make bags from baking or greaseproof paper, which will hold various-shaped tubes. You can also cut the tips off the bags to the size you require. These are ideal for small amounts of icing or chocolate.

Another option is to use a small plastic bag. Push the icing (or chocolate) into the corner of the bag, twist the bag around the icing, then snip the tip to the desired size and shape.

Icing tubes are made from metal or plastic, and can be bought from cake-decorating suppliers, some craft shops, supermarkets and cookware shops.

Non-stick rolling pins are available from cake-decorating and chefs' suppliers as well as cookware shops.

Candy thermometers, used to measure the temperature of syrup, are available from hardware and cookware shops.

We used strong double-pointed wooden toothpicks throughout this book.

Candy cake decorations, made from sugar, corn starch and vegetable gum, are assorted lettering, pictures and shapes used for decorating cakes. These can easily be found at your local supermarket.

Food colourings

We used good-quality edible gels and concentrated pastes, which are available from cake-decorating suppliers and some health-food stores.

It's best to add minuscule amounts (using a skewer or toothpick) to the icing until the desired colour is reached. Use care when handling food colourings as they stain.

Coloured icing can become darker or lighter on standing, so keep this in mind when decorating a cake ahead of time.

If you have the time, it's a good idea to experiment by colouring a small amount of the icing, then covering it with plastic wrap and allowing it to stand for a few hours to determine if the icing fades or darkens.

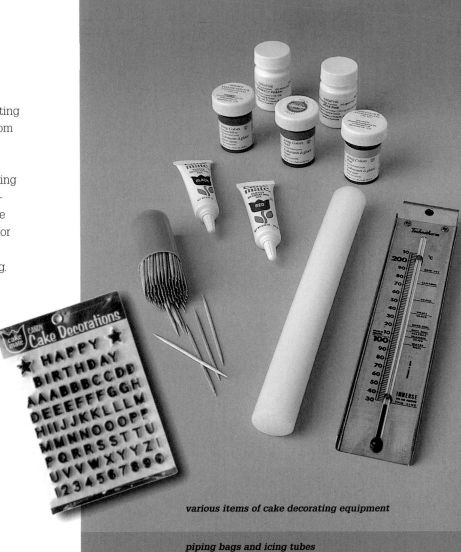

various items of cake decorating equipment

piping bags and icing tubes

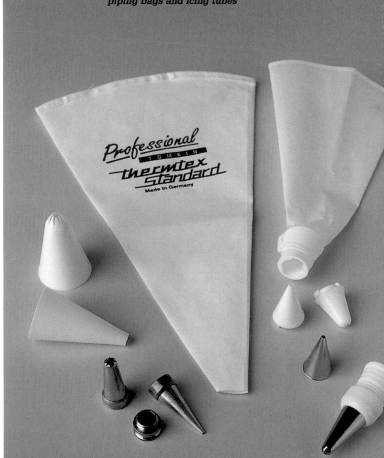

Fruit Sticks

Musk Sticks

jelly beans

chocolate coins

large teeth lolly

fruit Roll-Ups reel

fruit Roll-Ups

sour apple karate belt

white Life Savers

Jelly Tots

snakes

chocolate car

chocolate fish

raspberry strap

small hearts

Five Flavours Life Savers

Killer Python

Brite Crawlers

small jelly snake

fruit rings

chocolate ladybird

large hearts

candy cane

Fizzers

Carnival Pop

jubes

Chunky Raspberry Twister

spearmint leaves

Jaffa regular and giant

Screw Pop

orange segment jubes

small lollipop

black licorice rope

red licorice rope

red and green frogs

black licorice strap

black licorice twist

lollipop

M&M's

Smarties

Kool Fruits

Kool Mints

Fruit Fantasy Strawberries

bananas

mini M&M's

small gum balls

Oompas

raspberries

milk bottles

gum balls

Crazy Bananas

rainbow choc-chips

cake decorating moon and stars

Skittles

blue boiled lollies

strawberries and creams

licorice allsorts

jelly shark

coloured sprinkles

Tic Tacs

hundreds & thousands allsorts

Bo-Peeps

yellow sprinkles

orange sprinkles

mini musks

round licorice allsorts

coloured cachous

snowflakes

silver and gold sugar-covered almonds

Decorations

211

small
ice-cream
cone

crinkle
cut potato
chips

Sherbet
cone

potato straws

waffle cone

Coco Pops

Mentos

Rice
Bubbles

large
round
mints

pink and white
marshmallows

turkish delight

pink ice-cream wafer

Mallow Bakes

large white
marshmallow

pink fairy floss

coloured popcorn

Flake

Curly Wurly

chocolate finger biscuits

TeeVee Snacks

chocolate mint sticks

Dairy Milk rounds

milk chocolate Melts

Violet Crumble

chocolate freckles

chocolate sprinkles

After Dinner Mints

white chococolate Melts

chocolate thins

white Choc Bits

Clinkers

chocolate bullets

Chocolate Monte

Mint Slice

snowball

Mint Pattie

chocolate sea shells

Toblerone

chocolate-covered fruit and nuts

milk eating chocolate

white eating chocolate

dark eating chocolate

Cadbury

milk chocolate block

FaCTs + FIGuREs

Wherever you live, you'll be able to use our recipes with the help of these easy-to-follow conversions. While these conversions are approximate only, the difference between an exact and the approximate conversion of various liquid and dry measures is minimal and will not affect your cooking results.

DRY MEASURES

METRIC	IMPERIAL
15g	½oz
30g	1oz
60g	2oz
90g	3oz
125g	4oz (¼lb)
155g	5oz
185g	6oz
220g	7oz
250g	8oz (½lb)
280g	9oz
315g	10oz
345g	11oz
375g	12oz (¾lb)
410g	13oz
440g	14oz
470g	15oz
500g	16oz (1lb)
750g	24oz (1½lb)
1kg	32oz (2lb)

LIQUID MEASURES

METRIC	IMPERIAL
30ml	1 fluid oz
60ml	2 fluid oz
100ml	3 fluid oz
125ml	4 fluid oz
150ml	5 fluid oz (¼ pint/1 gill)
190ml	6 fluid oz
250ml	8 fluid oz
300ml	10 fluid oz (½ pint)
500ml	16 fluid oz
600ml	20 fluid oz (1 pint)
1000ml (1 litre)	1¾ pints

HELPFUL MEASURES

METRIC	IMPERIAL
3mm	⅛in
6mm	¼in
1cm	½in
2cm	¾in
2.5cm	1in
5cm	2in
6cm	2½in
8cm	3in
10cm	4in
13cm	5in
15cm	6in
18cm	7in
20cm	8in
23cm	9in
25cm	10in
28cm	11in
30cm	12in (1ft)

MEASURING EQUIPMENT

The difference between one country's measuring cups and another's is, at most, within a 2 or 3 teaspoon variance. (For the record, one Australian metric measuring cup holds approximately 250ml.) The most accurate way of measuring dry ingredients is to weigh them. When measuring liquids, use a clear glass or plastic jug with the metric markings. (One Australian metric tablespoon holds 20ml; one Australian metric teaspoon holds 5ml.)

HOW TO MEASURE

When using graduated metric measuring cups, shake dry ingredients loosely into the appropriate cup. Do not tap the cup on a bench or tightly pack the ingredients unless directed to do so. Level top of measuring cups and measuring spoons with a knife. When measuring liquids, place a clear glass or plastic jug with metric markings on a flat surface to check accuracy at eye level.

Note: North America, NZ and the UK use 15ml tablespoons. All cup and spoon measurements are level.

We use large eggs having an average weight of 60g.

OVEN TEMPERATURES

These oven temperatures are only a guide. Always check the manufacturer's manual.

	°C (CELSIUS)	°F (FAHRENHEIT)	GAS MARK
Very slow	120	250	½
Slow	140-150	275-300	1-2
Moderately slow	170	325	3
Moderate	180-190	350-375	4-5
Moderately hot	200	400	6
Hot	220-230	425-450	7-8
Very hot	240	475	9

Glossary

almond meal also known as ground almonds.

bean thread vermicelli also known as wun sen, or glass or cellophane noodles because they are transparent when cooked. White in colour, very delicate and fine. Must be soaked to soften before use; using them deep-fried requires no pre-soaking. Made from mung beans.

butter use salted or unsalted (sweet) butter; 125g is equal to 1 stick butter.

chenille sticks also known as pipe cleaners.

cocoa powder also just called cocoa; unsweetened, dried, roasted then ground cocoa beans.

COCONUT

   desiccated unsweetened, concentrated, dried finely shredded coconut.

   shredded thin strips of dried coconut.

CREAM

   fresh (minimum fat content 35%) also known as pure cream and pouring cream.

   thickened (minimum fat content 35%) a whipping cream containing a thickener.

cream of tartar the acid ingredient in baking powder; added to confectionery mixtures helps prevent sugar crystallising. Keeps frostings creamy and improves volume when beating egg whites.

Dolly Varden pan spherical, bombe-shaped cake pan.

FLOUR

   plain an all-purpose flour, made from wheat.

   self-raising plain flour sifted with baking powder in the proportion of 1 cup flour to 2 teaspoons baking powder.

fried noodles crispy egg noodles already deep-fried.

ice magic a chocolate coating for ice-cream; sets quickly.

ICE-CREAM
use good-quality ice-cream; ice-cream varieties differ from manufacturer to manufacturer depending on the quantities of air and fat incorporated into the mixture.

   neapolitan vanilla, strawberry and chocolate ice-cream.

jam also known as preserve or conserve.

jam rollettes also known as sponge rollettes; package cake product similar to small individual jelly roll.

jam rolls large jam rollettes.

lollies also known as sweets. Black licorice straps and 1m black licorice can be substituted for each other.

milk we used full-cream milk.

prunes commercially or sun-dried plums.

Rice Bubbles also known as Rice Crispies.

SUGAR

   caster also known as superfine or finely granulated table sugar.

   brown a soft, fine granulated sugar retaining molasses for its characteristic colour and flavour.

   icing sugar mixture also known as confectioners' sugar or powdered sugar; granulated sugar crushed together with a small amount (about 3%) of cornflour.

   pure icing sugar also known as confectioners' sugar or powdered sugar without the addition of cornflour.

   white we used coarse, granulated table sugar, unless otherwise specified.

vanilla extract vanilla beans that have been submerged in alcohol. Vanilla essence is not a suitable substitute.

vegetable oil any number of oils, sourced from plants rather than animal fats.

Index